THE HOUSE OF BERNARDA ALBA
AND OTHER PLAYS

BLOOD WEDDING
YERMA
THE HOUSE OF BERNARDA ALBA

FEDERICO GARCÍA LORCA

The New Authorized English Translations by
MICHAEL DEWELL *and* CARMEN ZAPATA

With an Introduction by
CHRISTOPHER MAURER

PENGUIN BOOKS

PENGUIN BOOKS

Published by the Penguin Group
Penguin Books Ltd, 80 Strand, London WC2R 0RL, England
Penguin Putnam Inc., 375 Hudson Street, New York, New York 10014, USA
Penguin Books Australia Ltd, 250 Camberwell Road, Camberwell, Victoria 3124, Australia
Penguin Books Canada Ltd, 10 Alcorn Avenue, Toronto, Ontario, Canada M4V 3B2
Penguin Books India (P) Ltd, 11 Community Centre, Panchsheel Park, New Delhi – 110 017, India
Penguin Books (NZ) Ltd, Cnr Rosedale and Airborne Roads, Albany, Auckland, New Zealand
Penguin Books (South Africa) (Pty) Ltd, 24 Sturdee Avenue, Rosebank 2196, South Africa

Penguin Books Ltd, Registered Offices: 80 Strand, London WC2R 0RL, England

www.penguin.com

Blood Wedding first published as *Bodas de sangre*, 1936
Yerma first published 1937
The House of Bernarda Alba first published as *La casa de Bernarda Alba*, 1946
These translations first published in the USA as *The Rural Trilogy* by Bantam Books, 1987
These translations, in revised form, first published in Great Britain by Penguin Books 1992
Reprinted in Penguin Classics 2001

3

Printed in England by Clays Ltd, St Ives plc
Set in 10/12.5 pt Monophoto Sabon

The Translators dedicate their work

to Margarita Galban
for asking them to do it,

to Nina Foch
for believing they could,

to Christopher Maurer
for making it so much better.

CONTENTS

INTRODUCTION

These three plays are often referred to as a 'rural trilogy' and as García Lorca's most mature and characteristic works. *Blood Wedding* (first performed in early 1933) and *Yerma* (1934) were, in fact, intended as the first plays in a 'trilogy of the Spanish earth', but that set of plays was never completed. *The House of Bernarda Alba* (finished in 1936; performed and published posthumously) does not form part of a cycle. Lorca was assassinated, at the age of 38, two months after he finished *Bernarda Alba*. He had no chance to meditate upon the final arrangement of his works.

Although these plays have long been considered classics of the modern European theatre, Lorca himself regarded them as the works of a beginner. As he worked on *Bernarda Alba*, which he had no opportunity to polish into a final draft, he told a Spanish journalist:

> I haven't yet reached the level of maturity ... I still consider myself a true novice, and I'm still learning my profession ... One has to ascend one step at a time ... [One shouldn't] demand of my nature, my spiritual and intellectual development, something that no author can give until much later ... My work has just begun.

Nor did Lorca consider these plays to be especially 'characteristic' of his own theatre. Since 1920, the year of his first production (a fable about insects entitled *The Butterfly's Evil Spell*), he had experimented incessantly, both cultivating traditional genres (the puppet play, the historical verse-drama, farce) and challenging them. At a crucial moment in his development as a dramatist he would identify two early experimental plays, *The Public* (begun in 1930) and *Once Five Years Pass* (finished in 1931) as more truly 'his' than the rest of his works. He said that he had written his other plays – including *Blood Wedding* and *Yerma* – 'in order to show [my] personality and to earn respect' within the mainstream theatre. Such comments were meant to remind the public that his theatre had already taken off in other directions; that he hoped to go on breaking new ground; and that he was *not* to be classified as a writer of 'folk tragedies'.

There was widespread agreement in the 1920s that the Spanish theatre was undergoing a deep crisis, both aesthetic and economic. A stream of books and newspaper articles deplored the mediocrity of playwrights, the ignorance of critics, actors and audiences, and the indifference of government officials. Few writers were more aware of this crisis than Lorca. In 1929, from his dormitory room at Columbia University, where he was working on *Poet in New York*, he wrote to his parents: 'one must think of the theatre of the future. Everything that now exists in Spain is dead. Either the theatre changes radically, or it dies away forever. There is no other solution.'

In 1929 Lorca had not yet become famous as a playwright. Only two of his plays had been performed, and he was chiefly known as the author of *The Gypsy Ballads* (1928). What he brought back from New York, where he often went to the theatre, was a sense of urgency and perspective, and the feeling that he himself could help to revitalize the Spanish stage. It was in America that he began work on *The Public* (never performed during his lifetime), a rebellious drama which called for the abolition of conventional theatre.

In fact, the Spanish stage was far from 'dead', and reform was well under way. Two writers, Miguel de Unamuno (1846–1936) and Ramón del Valle-Inclán (1866–1936) had protested indignantly, earlier in the 1920s, against the banality of the Spanish theatre, and both were to leave a deep impression on Lorca.

The ascetic Unamuno tried to strip both the text and stage of unnecessary ornament and to explore the same problems that he had confronted in his philosophical essays and novels: artistic creation, faith, free will, personal identity. Calling for a return to the austerity and intensity of classical tragedy, Unamuno rewrote the myths of Medea and Phaedra and struggled without success to find a modern expression for dramatic fate. In *Yerma*, a play in which, as Lorca once remarked, 'nothing happens', one feels Unamuno's legacy: his disgust with a theatre and a nascent film industry dominated by 'squirrelish action', as well as his insistence on emotional intensity.

More prolific and influential than Unamuno, Valle-Inclán experimented both with re-creating Shakespearian tragedy and with new forms of tragicomedy. The greatest of Valle-Inclán's later plays (the ones he called *esperpentos*) grow from the simple intuition that what seems tragic to us – a spouse's infidelity, for example – is often regarded by others as comical or grotesque. Lorca develops that theme in two of his farces: *The Shoemaker's Prodigious Wife* and *The Love of Don Perlimplín for Belisa in Their Garden*. There are occasional verbal echoes of Valle-Inclán's works both in Lorca's poems and in his plays, and Valle's trilogy *Comedias bárbaras* contained three elements that deeply interested the younger playwright: their rural setting, their use of theatrical space, and their peculiar vision of tragedy. Like Lorca, Valle-Inclán had the eye of a painter with a keen sense of space and colour. Both writers set many of their plays not in aristocratic salons or drawing rooms but in a highly stylized countryside. Valle-Inclán was an implacable enemy of mediocre actors, and he must also have impressed Lorca by his refusal to compromise with the commercial theatre.

Another aspect of Valle-Inclán's work seems relevant here: his fascination with melodrama. Arguing that Spaniards have a special penchant for shouting, Valle-Inclán wrote his dialogue in fragmented, exclamatory language, and drew ironically on the melodramatic tradition of José Echegaray and others. Unlike Lorca's, his intentions were satirical. But there is more than a hint of melodrama in Lorca's own theatre, especially in *Blood Wedding*, the very title of which hearkens back to Echegaray.

Neither Unamuno nor Valle-Inclán had the artistic gifts or

practical skills they needed to *realize* their vision and produce their own works successfully. The multifaceted Lorca was able to draw costume designs and stage settings, to arrange music for his plays, and even, on occasion, to accompany the actors at the piano. He also trained himself thoroughly as a stage director and supervised rehearsals and performances. In New York he had come into contact with amateur theatre groups and professional repertory companies. A year after his return to Spain, with the end of the Primo de Rivera dictatorship and the declaration of the Second Spanish Republic (1931), he was able to form his own amateur group, attract government funding, and use the experience as an apprenticeship in theatrical production. His experience with La Barraca, a troupe of student actors who gave free performances of classical Spanish theatre for rural audiences throughout Spain, forced him to grapple with practical problems of stagecraft, the training of actors, and the adaptation of classical works. His travels with La Barraca also led him to meditate on two questions which concerned him deeply throughout his life: the impact of theatre on society and the needs and expectations of different sorts of audiences.

A deep concern for social justice is evident even in Lorca's earliest works. But no doubt the trip to New York (his first encounter with urban masses) and the social turmoil of republican Spain brought that concern to the fore. There is hardly anything in *Blood Wedding* that might be construed as 'social criticism', but by 1935 Lorca had declared himself an 'enthusiastic, devoted follower of the theatre of social action'. He now defined theatre as

> a school of laughter and lamentation, an open tribunal where the people can introduce old and mistaken mores as evidence, and can use living examples to explain eternal norms of the heart ... The theatre is an extremely useful instrument for the edification of a country, and the barometer that measures its greatness or decline. A sensitive theatre, well oriented in all its

branches, from tragedy to vaudeville, can alter a people's sensibility in just a few years, while a decadent theatre where hooves have taken the place of wings can cheapen and lull to sleep an entire nation.

When Lorca attacks the norms of theatrical realism and the expectations of middle-class audiences, one senses that, emboldened by Surrealism, he is questioning not only an aesthetic current but certain aspects of urban, bourgeois morality: its supposed indifference to suffering, its implacable hostility to deviant forms of behaviour, its fear of death and of the forces of nature, its mistrust of fantasy and of the artistic imagination.

Blood Wedding had won almost universal praise for having restored tragic poetry to the Spanish stage, but *Yerma* was harshly criticized by the right-wing press as a subversive attack on 'decency' and traditional 'Spanish values'. *Bernarda Alba* was not performed during Lorca's lifetime, but its very subtitle, 'A Drama of Women in the Villages of Spain', implies a critique of the status of women in male-dominated Spanish society. An introductory note declares that *Bernarda Alba* is intended as 'a photographic documentary'. Other projects on controversial social themes, from homosexuality to pacifism, were in preparation when Lorca was murdered in Granada in August, 1936.

Poetry and Music

There are two areas in particular in which Lorca's theatre differs radically from that of his predecessors: his idea of poetic drama, and the musical nature of his works.

'Theatre', Lorca remarked in 1936, is 'poetry that rises from the book and becomes human enough to talk and shout, weep and despair.' In Lorca's work, drama and poetry seem inseparable. His poetry often has the dramatic quality that he admired in traditional Spanish songs and narrative ballads, and his drama has the metaphorical density, the attention to rhythm, the ring of 'memorable speech' one usually associates with poetry. In each of these plays, images, metaphors and symbols form a coherent whole, a poetic system whose meaning cannot be paraphrased.

The distinction between prose and verse was not an essential part of Lorca's aesthetic. Form and genre often seem almost accidental, a means to an end. On occasion, he describes prose pieces and even drawings as 'poems'. *Yerma* is proudly subtitled 'A Tragic *Poem* in Three Acts and Six Scenes'. Without ever theorizing about poetic drama, Lorca knew that it did not necessarily entail the use of verse. It was, simply, the drama written by poets: 'The theatre which has endured has always been that of poets.' That guiding ideal, which bore its first fruit in *Blood Wedding*, was something new in Spanish theatre. No Spanish playwright since Lope de Vega or Calderón de la Barca had appealed so forcefully to the poetic imagination of so many people, from such a wide cross-section of society, in Spain and abroad. None has done so since Lorca's death.

In the 1920s and 1930s the Spanish theatre was not entirely friendly to what Lorca understood as poetic drama, although it was remarkably tolerant of verse. Historical drama, for example, was still being written in verse by Eduardo Marquina (1879–1946) and others. Lorca had contributed to this tradition in *Mariana Pineda* (1927), the story of a woman executed in Granada, in the early nineteenth century, for having taken part in a liberal conspiracy against the tyrannical Ferdinand VII. What *was* unusual (and revolutionary) in Lorca's later plays was the use of both prose and verse within the same play, as in *Blood Wedding*. No major Spanish writer since the age of Romanticism had combined the two so boldly and gracefully.

In *Blood Wedding*, Lorca once remarked, prose and verse have their own distinct functions:

> Well-wrought, free prose can soar to expressive heights, freeing us from the confinement and rigidity of metre. Let us welcome verse at moments when the excitement and disposition of the

theme demand it, only then. You can see that, in *Blood Wedding*, verse does not appear with any intensity or at any length until the wedding scene. Then, with the scene in the forest and in the last scene in the work, it takes complete command of the stage.

The use of verse decreases in *Yerma* and is almost entirely absent from *Bernarda Alba*, where Maria Josefa's lyrics acquire special intensity because they interrupt the 'prose' of the other characters. As he worked on *Bernarda Alba*, Lorca told a friend that it had 'not a single drop of poetry'. But, arguably, *Yerma* and *Bernarda Alba* are no less poetic than *Blood Wedding*. Together they are an important part of Lorca's challenge to Western theatre: the sense that, in our own age, 'poetic theatre' need not be written in verse, be at odds with realism, or remind us of the theatre of the past (none of these plays sounds at all archaic in Spanish).

The American critic Francis Fergusson, one of the first to recognize Lorca's achievement, observed in 1957 that Lorca 'wrote poetic drama very much as Yeats and Eliot have taught us to understand it; yet his plays are neither cultish nor middlebrow-Ersatz: they are theatre-poetry which lives naturally on the modern stage.' Lorca himself admired and imitated Synge: *Blood Wedding* has reminded many readers of *Riders to the Sea*. He also knew some of Eliot's poetry. But he does not seem to have followed the dramatic experimentation of either Eliot or Yeats, and never theorized about theatre poetry. 'The greater the poet,' he once remarked ingenuously, 'the greater his theatre.'

A second distinctive characteristic of Lorca's theatre is music. As a young man he had studied the piano and had tried his hand at composition; a few of his early pieces are conserved in the Fundación Federico García Lorca, Madrid. It was only after the death of his piano teacher in 1916 that he turned from classical music to literature. His enduring passion for music – folk, popular, classical, contemporary – was nurtured in the 1920s by Manuel de Falla, a close friend of the Lorca family. With Falla, Federico wrote the text of an unfinished comic opera (*Lola, the Actress*). Lorca's passion for music was fed by other composers, performers and musicologists of his own generation: Adolfo Salazar, Ernesto Halffter, the guitarists Andrés Segovia and Regino Sáinz de la Maza, the dancer and singer Encarnación López Júlvez, 'La Argentinita'.

Not surprisingly, both his poems and plays try to reconcile literature and music, at first by using musical imagery (e.g., 'the fermata of the half moon') and later by drawing on musical structures, as in *Suites* (1921–3), a book of poetic sequences several of which take the form of a theme and variations. Both as stage director and as a writer of dialogue Lorca is aware of the crucial importance of rhythm:

> One needs to rehearse for a long time, and very carefully, to achieve the rhythm that ought to govern the performance of a dramatic work. To me, this is very important. An actor cannot wait a second too long before opening a door. A flaw of this sort has a deplorable effect. It is as though, when one were interpreting a symphony, the melody or some other musical effect were to come in at the wrong time. The hardest thing to achieve in the theatre is to have the work begin, develop and end in accordance with an established rhythm.

Lorca's vision of theatre draws upon ballet and other forms of dance, and in his own work as a director he devoted much attention to the stylization of movement. In 1933, on staging a series of Spanish popular songs in Buenos Aires, he spoke of the need to devote attention

> to the human body, which is completely forgotten in the theatre. We must present a festival of the body, from the toes . . . to the hair. Ruling over all this we have the actor's eyes, indicating what is going on inside him. The body, its harmony, its rhythm, has been forgotten . . . We must restore value to the body in the theatre. That is what I am trying to do.

Nowhere is musical form more apparent than in *Blood Wedding*, where the characters' speech is 'orchestrated' in a highly stylized, rhythmic manner that sometimes borders on liturgical chant. Lorca's brother Francisco, who wrote brilliant essays on each of these plays, has remembered how concerned the poet was about the rhythm of Act II scene i, where the Bride leaves for the wedding: 'The bride is awakening / On the morning of the wedding!' That scene, he writes, is 'fragmented by many characters entering and leaving, at different heights on the stage, with the alternating play of male and female voices, speaking lines of extraordinary rhythmic complexity. Federico interrupted the rehearsals frequently, exclaiming, "It has got to be mathematically precise."' The actress Josefina Díaz de Artigas, who played the Bride in the 1933 Madrid première, remembers that Lorca staged that scene rather like the conductor of an orchestra, 'so that there wouldn't be a single voice that didn't blend with the others . . . He combined the voices, their special timbres and strengths, as a composer puts together sounds. It was an extraordinary effort. He would shout "Not you! Your voice is too shrill! *You* try! I need a deep voice. I need a fresh voice here."'

There is ample textual and biographical evidence to support this. For example, in a production of *Blood Wedding* in New York during Lorca's lifetime (1935), lines assigned to the Mother and Wife in the final scene are interchanged, as though characterization mattered less than tonal harmony. The translator, who consulted with Lorca, wrote on his manuscript: 'Federico thinks that instead of Novia [the Bride], the womenfolk like a choir should speak these words. But he did not dare to do so in Madrid, on account of poor work of second-rate actors.'

We know, in addition, that, as Lorca wrote the play during the summer of 1932, he listened obsessively to two records: one of the *cante jondo* singer Tomás Pavón, and one of a cantata by Bach. Though it is impossible to identify that cantata, it is tempting to suppose that the wedding scene in *Blood Wedding* was inspired in part by cantata no. 140 ('Wachet auf! ruft uns die Stimme'), a joyful celebration of the symbolic marriage of the daughters of Jerusalem with Christ: '"Wake up," cries the voice of the sentinel from his tower. "Wake up, oh Jerusalem!"' What we hear in the cantata, writes W. G. Whittaker (and his words are equally relevant to *Blood Wedding*), is 'an amazing scene of excitement and confusion, people rushing to and fro, sounds of voices coming from all quarters of the streets, while the serene and divine announcement of the coming of the Bridegroom peals above the mêlée' (*The Cantatas of J. S. Bach. Sacred and Secular*). Lorca is working with dramatic components somewhat analogous to those of the cantata. In Act II scene i of *Blood Wedding*, we find choral and individual singing as well as short, spoken prose passages. In the first movement of the cantata, the sopranos' call, '*Wachet auf!*', is imitated by the altos, tenors and basses. García Lorca's use of a strikingly similar refrain ('The bride is awakening / On the morning of the wedding!') is sung and spoken by different men, women and children, in a sort of imitative entry. Not surprisingly, the cantata has been compared to a theatrical work:

> The accompanying voices are lively, psychologically apt, and at one point . . . even impatient with the slow pace of the hymn tune. The accompanying voices will do most of their energetic urging-on in carefully spaced bursts of fervour. As if this were a mass scene on the theatre stage, Bach changes the order of their mostly imitative entrances as often as possible.
>
> (Gerard Herz, ed., *Cantata No. 140,*
> *Wachet auf! ruft uns die Stimme*).

No less important than the rhythmic stylization upon which Lorca insisted as director are two other musical elements: the songs and dances performed by the characters, and the background music. The songs of the washerwomen in *Yerma* or the spinners in *Blood Wedding* are reminiscent of Spanish folk tunes. They are also meant to suggest the choruses of Greek tragedy, commenting on the action and revealing something of the psychology of the characters. 'What interests me most about my drama,' Lorca said of *Yerma*, 'is the process of [Yerma's] obsession. She speaks the same way, from the time she enters until she leaves, and I have taken care to accompany her with a monotonous musicality.'

Lorca also used music as a way of weaning his audiences from expectations of realism. What he says of the music in his farce *The Shoemaker's Prodigious Wife* is applicable also to *Blood Wedding*: 'The use of music allows me to make the scene less realistic, and do away with the audience's impression that what is going on is "really happening", permitting me to raise things to the level of poetry.' There is a good example of this technique at the beginning of Act III of *Blood Wedding*. The stage directions say: 'A forest. Night. Great moist tree-trunks. A murky atmosphere. Two violins are playing.' It is not known what music those violins were playing, but a translator's note in the manuscript of the New York production reveals what the audience listened to in Madrid in 1934, as it waited for that act to begin: 'andante of Brandenburg concerto of Bach. They used a disk in Madrid. It has to sound from afar. When curtain rises, the Three Woodcutters are on stage, without moving.' Presumably, this would have been the *andante* from the second Brandenburg concerto. Remembering two different moments in the play, Lorca later remarked that '*Blood Wedding* ... is taken from Bach ... That third act, the scene in the woods, the moon, the business of death prowling around: all this is in the Bach cantata that I had.' Few plays are more thoroughly musical than *Blood Wedding*; several recent versions dispense entirely with the text.

Tragedy and Elegy

In the wake of Unamuno and Valle-Inclán, but in a profoundly original way, Lorca declared his intention to 'return to tragedy. Our dramatic tradition obliges us to do so.' For Lorca, tragedy entails formal elements like the use of a chorus. But above all it involves creating an illusion of fate or destiny, of 'necessariness', the suggestion that men and women are at the mercy of elemental forces which shape their lives in ways they barely comprehend. Tragedy is woven from the 'necessary' speech of poetry (the illusion that there is *no other way* to express what is being said) and from 'necessary' action (the illusion of destiny). This feeling of inevitability must be coupled with mystery. 'Only mystery makes us live,' Lorca wrote beneath one of his drawings. In his view, no tragedy can be fully explained. The essence of both poetry and tragedy lies in mystery, and the mystery of Lorca's plays is not generated by abstract ideas or by suspenseful action, but by the resonance and ambiguity of his poetic imagery, imagery firmly rooted in the senses.

Lorca's images flee from abstraction and seem to arise from material reality. Emotions, for example, are often expressed as physiological phenomena:

> How can it be that something as small as a pistol or a knife can destroy a man who is like a bull? I'll never be quiet. The months go by, and the desperation stings my eyes and the very tips of my hair!

> Every time I mention her, I feel as if I'd been struck on the forehead with a rock.

Yerma's solitude finds expression in simple images like these:

> I want to drink water and there's no glass and no water! I want to walk up the hill, and I have no feet! I want to embroider my petticoats, and I can't find the thread!

Leonardo describes what he felt when the Bride married another man:

> The silver pins of your wedding
> Were making my blood turn black.
> The dream was filling my flesh
> With bitter, choking weeds!

Water and weeds, hill, pins, thread . . . however mysterious its meaning, Lorca's imagery arises from what can be seen, touched, smelled or heard. 'A poet must be a professor of the five bodily senses,' he once observed in a lecture on Góngora. Throughout his theatre, general ideas like fate or death became almost tangible.

There is also, as Francisco García Lorca has noticed, a movement in the opposite direction. As with those characters whose 'generic' names remind us that they are eternal types, particular objects – a horse, an arm, the knife, the moon – come to seem universal, essential, prototypical. While searching for the Bride, the Bridegroom remarks: 'See this arm? Well, it is not my arm – it is the arm of my brother and my father and of everyone in my family who is dead! And it has so much power that it can pull this tree up by the roots, if it wants!'

This movement from the particular towards the universal helps produce an illusion of tragic fate. Tragedy involves a search for the essential, eternal qualities of things, as in the Maid's stunningly simple definition of marriage: 'It's a shining bed, and a man, and a woman!' Or the Mother's: 'One man, some children – and a wall six feet thick, to shut out everything else.' Or Bernarda's view of the sexes: 'A needle and thread for females: a mule and a whip for males.' This is a world of 'men that are men, wheat that is wheat', where things recover their essences.

For all its sensual immediacy, Lorca's imagery makes a bold appeal to the subconscious. Deploring the sober rationalism and 'objectivity' of modern American poetry, Robert Bly writes: 'Lorca's poems have many things in them sharply observed ("black doves puttering the putrid waters"), but they also have images, also passion, wild leaps, huge arsenic lobsters falling out of the sky.' Lorca does not delve into the subconscious in the manner of Freud, as did other Spanish playwrights of the 1920s and 30s, or in the manner of Surrealism. He draws on magical thinking, which often resembles that of ancient naturalistic religions. Such 'magic' is everywhere in *Yerma*. Conception, for example, is no scientific matter; it is something breathed into the ear, or something that fills the voice, or something drawn directly from the earth: 'Many nights I go out . . . barefoot, to feel the earth under my feet, and I don't know why.' The religious historian Alvaro Alvarez de Miranda has called attention to many of these primitivistic elements: the overwhelming presence of the moon, as giver and taker of life; the deeply felt images of blood and of water; the ritual veneration of the knife.

In his search for what is tragic and essential, Lorca drew skilfully on a millennial tradition. One of his favourite images of Andalusia is that of an historical palimpsest of pre-Roman, classical, Christian, Jewish and Islamic elements. All three of these tragedies allude to contemporary events as well, altered and re-created by the poet. *Blood Wedding* has its origin in a newspaper account of a murder committed the day before a wedding in Níjar, in the southeastern province of Almería. It is Almería, where cave dwelling is not unknown, which suggested the arid landscapes of that play, 'hard as a landscape on a piece of ceramic folk art'. There are numerous 'factual' details in *The House of Bernarda Alba*. An Alba family lived near the García Lorcas in the Andalusian village of Asquerosa, and, not surprisingly, some of the characters in the play – Bernarda, Poncia and others – were suggested by real people. And yet, as happens in Lorca's poetry, modern elements like these are credibly transformed into something very ancient. The fertility rites in *Yerma* are based in part on the yearly pilgrimage to Moclín, in the province of Granada, but Lorca easily convinces us of their wholly pagan character. The girls spinning wool in *Blood Wedding* can be justified realistically, but they are also meant to remind us of the Parcae.

There is still another way, beyond the ones already noted, in which Lorca's dramas are grounded in mystery: the motivations of his characters. Critics have often tried to reduce these plays to antithetical formulae, or to study them as variations on a single theme. All three plays appear to represent a struggle between freedom and repression, or a conflict between the individual and society, or between natural law and social law. If Yerma cannot bear a child, it is, some argue, because a rigid code of societal honour prevents her from abandoning Juan or taking advantage of the fertility rites described in Act III. More or less the same struggle is played out in *Blood Wedding*: the Bride succumbs to her passion, evading what is socially acceptable (marriage with the Bridegroom), and this leads to death. Bernarda's obsession with 'What the neighbours will say' contributes, without a doubt, to the suicide of Adela.

In all three dramas, characters focus obsessively on a single object: Yerma yearns for a child; the Bride longs for Leonardo; Adela, for Pepe el Romano. And in all three plays, desire is frustrated violently and fatally by social forces. Authority appears to triumph over freedom, society over personal instinct, the social law over the deeper imperatives of nature. This message seems especially apt from a playwright whose own sexuality caused him much suffering and whose life was cut short by the advent of political repression. *The House of Bernarda Alba* has often been read as a premonition of the Franco regime, and hearing Bernarda's pathetic final words – 'Silence! Silence, I said! Silence!' – one cannot help but remember the censorship that would descend upon Spanish liberal thought, and upon Lorca's own work, for several decades (the play was long banned in Spain).

The 'social' interpretation of these plays is certainly justifiable. Lorca himself encouraged it, both from within the plays and in public statements like those already mentioned. *The House of Bernarda Alba* roundly condemns authoritarianism and the class system which perpetuates it. 'The poor are like animals,' Bernarda remarks. 'They seem to be made of other substances.' And yet the social reading is grossly inadequate. There *is* a fundamental antithesis in Lorca's work, but it is even more inclusive than the struggle between the individual and society. From his earliest works Lorca is an elegist, and the *social* implications of these three plays are but one manifestation of the duality involved in all elegy. Broadly considered, elegy compares two modes of being: presence and absence: what is and what was; how things are and how they might have been.

The central theme of all of Lorca's work is, indeed, desire. All of his characters *want* something. But the object of desire is invisible, shadowy, like Pepe el Romano. The plays do not merely suggest that society frustrates our intimate desires and instincts; they suggest that those desires and instincts can never be clearly identified. Lorca's characters are unhappy and 'tragic' not because society keeps them from attaining their object or reaching their destination, but because they cannot fully understand what it is that they want.

The same dilemma is apparent everywhere in Lorca's poetry and in his very conception of life. In his meditation upon the *pena negra* (literally 'black sorrow' or 'black pain') that is mentioned in the lyrics of Andalusian folk music, or *cante jondo*, Lorca had insisted that such pain has no apparent cause. It is, simply, 'incurable pain, the black pain we cannot get rid of except by taking a knife and opening a deep buttonhole in our left side.' What Lorca says of Soledad Montoya, the gypsy protagonist of one of his *Ballads*, seems applicable also to the characters in his plays:

> The pain of Soledad Montoya is the root of the Andalusian people. It is not anguish, because in this pain one can smile; nor does it blind, for it never produces weeping. It is a longing without object, a keen love of nothing, with the certainty that death (the eternal care of Andalusia) is breathing behind the door.

Many of Lorca's most memorable poems give expression to this blind longing, e.g. the 'Qasida of the Rose', from his last great elegiac book, *The Divan at Tamarit*:

> The rose
> was not searching for the dawn.
> Almost eternal on its branch,
> it was seeking something else.
>
> The rose
> was not searching for knowledge or shadow.
> Enclosure of flesh and dream
> it was seeking something else.

The rose
was not seeking the rose.
Immobile in the sky
it was seeking something else!

That 'something else' lies beyond language. Poetry and drama are unable to name it, only gesture towards it. They *are* the gesture: a mysterious, stylized gesture towards meaning.

The signs of this indeterminacy are found in all three of these plays, but are most apparent in *Yerma*. What is it that Yerma longs for? Her longing for a child is, somehow, more than that. It is an almost metaphysical search for completion, for the meaning of her own life. When her husband Juan tells her to stop fretting and to resign herself to her barrenness, he calls attention not only to his own insensitivity but to the indeterminacy of her desire: 'I can no longer put up with this constant grieving over obscure things, unreal things made of thin air ... Over things that have not happened and that neither you nor I can control.' By the final act of the play, Yerma's longing for a child has given way to something much more difficult to define. It is the 'keen love of nothing', the uncentred desire, of Soledad Montoya. Offered the chance to leave Juan and move in with someone who can give her a child, Yerma protests: 'I'm like a parched field big enough to hold a thousand teams of oxen plowing, and what you give me is a little glass of water from the well! Mine is pain that is no longer of my flesh!'

The ultimate antithesis, then, is not that of society and the individual, but of presence (the realm of reality) and absence (the realm of the imagination). Yerma's tragedy is *not* that society keeps her from fulfilling a biological urge or realizing herself fully. It is that she can desire, can imagine and feel what is absent, while her husband cannot. 'All I care about is what I can hold in my hands,' Juan says, 'what I can see with my eyes!' Beyond its appeal for justice, for freedom, and for sexual and social equality, Lorca's theatre is a passionate defence of poetry and of the imagination. His characters' search for meaning parallels that of the reader. The result is dramatic poetry or poetic drama unsurpassed by any writer of our time.

Christopher Maurer

Vanderbilt University, 1991

A NOTE ON THE TRANSLATION

Carmen Zapata and I began to translate Lorca's plays in 1977, not by choice but of necessity. Carmen was spending her off-camera hours creating a new Los Angeles theatre company, the Bilingual Foundation of the Arts, a group in which the actors played their roles one night in Spanish and the next in English. Carmen was eager to get her teeth into the extraordinary repertory of female roles in the Lorca canon, but there were no translations that she felt were playable.

So we set to work to make a translation of *Bodas de sangre* that would be accepted by bilingual actors and audiences. Six months later, and four weeks into their Spanish-language rehearsals, we gave the actors our 'final' draft. What a revelation! Immersed in the original, the actors had all sorts of problems with our translation. They were thinking and feeling in Spanish, but being asked to speak in English. When good actors just couldn't force out our words, we knew that changes were called for. Hundreds of changes, from single words to complete sentences. Occasionally, the actors themselves could tell us what was needed; more often, we had to be there at the moment when they stumbled, then talk to them during a rehearsal break, retire to the lobby to talk through our own solution, and then scribble away back in our seats, rewriting and rewriting.

The process continued all the way through three more weeks of rehearsals and *Blood Wedding*'s two-month run. After closing night we began our own work sessions, and we prepared a new draft for yet another kind of script try-out. This time we would mount an English-only staged reading, casting monolingual actors who didn't know the original, and we would give performances for an English-speaking audience. By then we both knew that we'd stumbled on to something – a way to forge play translations out of the theatre's long process of readings and try-outs and rewrites of new plays, that series of crucibles from which original scripts emerge as playable dramas.

As master translator Gregory Rabassa once told me, 'Good dialogue is like a good pair of boots: it takes a little spit to make it shine.' Over the years, with two more productions, we further revised *Blood Wedding*, and went through much the same process with *Yerma* and *The House of Bernarda Alba*.

Many people encouraged us in our work. The playwright's sister Isabel García Lorca and his nephew Manuel Fernández-Montesinos expressed their interest in having better English translations of these plays, and gave their authorization to these versions. The National Endowment for the Arts in Washington and the Del Amo Foundation in Los Angeles provided funding. Christopher Maurer painstakingly checked our original against reliable Spanish editions of these plays (ed. Mario Hernández, *Obras*, Madrid, Alianza Editorial, 1981), and made a number of suggestions. Thanks to him, this edition has been thoroughly revised since its original appearance (*The Rural Trilogy*, Bantam Books, 1987).

Our *Blood Wedding* won a cornucopia of awards in its 1984 revival, and *Yerma* was given a 1983 *Drama-Logue* Award for stage writing, the first time a translation had won it. I trust that our approach – continuous revision, tried out on live actors – is consistent with Lorca's vision of theatre as a 'live' phenomenon which evolves *on stage*.

When an Italian journalist asked Lorca in 1935 whether or not he intended to publish *his works*, he broke into laughter.

Publish? I don't publish my plays, I have them recited and performed. Plays are made to be felt in the theatre. They should last as long as the performance does, that's enough. If the audience wants to see them again, they can come back to life, one time or twenty, or fifty, but that is that. This is what makes the theatre so lovely: as soon as it is created, it disappears.

My dearest hope is that reading and seeing Lorca in English will encourage people to read his poems and see his plays in their incomparable Spanish original.

Michael Dewell

Los Angeles, 1991

BLOOD WEDDING

A Tragedy in Three Acts and Seven Scenes

Cast of Characters

THE BRIDEGROOM

THE BRIDEGROOM'S MOTHER

THE BRIDE

THE BRIDE'S FATHER

LEONARDO

LEONARDO'S WIFE

LEONARDO'S MOTHER-IN-LAW

THE MAID

THE NEIGHBOUR

THE MOON

DEATH

THREE WOODCUTTERS

TWO YOUNG MEN

GIRL

THREE GIRLS

LITTLE GIRL

THREE GUESTS

A WOMAN

NEIGHBOURS

ACT ONE

Scene 1

The room is painted yellow.

BRIDEGROOM [*entering*]: Mother?

MOTHER: Yes.

BRIDEGROOM: I'm going.

MOTHER: Where?

BRIDEGROOM: To the vineyard. [*He starts to go.*]

MOTHER: Wait.

BRIDEGROOM: Do you need something?

MOTHER: Son, your breakfast!

BRIDEGROOM: Never mind. I'll eat some grapes. Give me the knife.

MOTHER: What for?

BRIDEGROOM [*laughing*]: To cut them with.

MOTHER [*muttering as she looks for it*]: The knife! The knife! Damn all of them! And the monster who invented them!

BRIDEGROOM: Let's change the subject.

MOTHER: And the shotguns and the pistols and the smallest knife – and even the pitchfork and the hoe!

BRIDEGROOM: Enough!

MOTHER: Anything that can cut into a man's body! A beautiful man, with life like a flower in his mouth, who goes out to the vineyards or to his own olive groves, because they are his, inherited . . .

BRIDEGROOM [*lowering his head*]: Mother, be quiet!

MOTHER: . . . and that man does not return. Or if he does, it's only to have a palm placed over him or a dish of rock salt, so his body won't swell. I don't know how you dare to carry a knife on you! Or why I allow this serpent inside the cupboard!

BRIDEGROOM: Haven't you said enough?

3

MOTHER: If I lived a hundred years, I would talk of nothing else! First, your father. To me he smelled like carnations, and I enjoyed him only three short years. Then your brother. Is it fair? How can it be that something as small as a pistol or a knife can destroy a man who is like a bull? I'll never be quiet. The months go by, and the desperation stings my eyes and the very tips of my hair!

BRIDEGROOM [*loudly*]: Can't we be done with it?

MOTHER: No, we can't be done with it! Can anyone bring me back your father? Or your brother? And then there is the prison. What is a prison? People eat there, they smoke there, they play their music there. My dead ones, covered with weeds, silent, turned to dust. Two men who were like two geraniums! The killers, in prison, alive and well, gazing at the mountains.

BRIDEGROOM: Do you want me to kill them?

MOTHER: No. . . . If I talk about it, it's because – how can I *not* talk about it, watching you go out that door? I don't want you to carry a knife. I just . . . I just wish you wouldn't go out to the fields.

BRIDEGROOM [*laughing*]: Mother!

MOTHER: How I wish you had been a girl! You wouldn't be going down to the stream now. And we would be embroidering linens and little wool dogs.

BRIDEGROOM [*takes her by the arm and laughs*]: Mother, what if I took you with me to the vineyard?

MOTHER: What would an old woman do in the vineyard! Would you hide me under the vine leaves?

BRIDEGROOM [*lifting her up in his arms*]: Old woman! Old, old woman! Old, old, old woman!

MOTHER: Your father did take me. That's good stock, good blood! Your grandfather left a son on every corner. That I like – men that are men, wheat that is wheat.

BRIDEGROOM: And me, mother?

MOTHER: What about you?

BRIDEGROOM: Do I have to tell you again?

4

MOTHER [*serious*]: Oh!

BRIDEGROOM: Does it bother you?

MOTHER: No.

BRIDEGROOM: What is it?

MOTHER: I don't know myself. All of a sudden, like this, it always surprises me. I know she's a good girl. That's true, isn't it? Quiet, hard-working. She bakes her bread and sews her skirts – and yet, every time I mention her, I feel as if I'd been struck on the forehead with a rock.

BRIDEGROOM: That's nonsense!

MOTHER: It's not nonsense. I'll be left alone! You're all I have now, and it makes me sad that you'll be leaving.

BRIDEGROOM: But you will come with us.

MOTHER: No. I can't leave your father and your brother alone here. I have to go to them every morning. And if I go away, one of the Felixes might easily die. One of that family of killers! And they might bury him right next to them. And that – never! Never! Because I will dig him up with my fingernails! And all by myself, I will smash him against the wall!

BRIDEGROOM [*loudly*]: Back to that again!!

MOTHER: Forgive me. [*Pause*] How long have you been seeing her?

BRIDEGROOM: Three years. I was finally able to buy the vineyard.

MOTHER: Three years. She used to see someone else, didn't she?

BRIDEGROOM: I don't know – I don't think so. Girls have to look carefully at who they are going to marry.

MOTHER: Yes. I didn't look at anyone. I looked at your father, and when they killed him, I looked at the wall in front of me. One woman with one man, and that's it.

BRIDEGROOM: You know my fiancée's a good girl.

MOTHER: I don't doubt it. Anyway, I'm sorry I don't know what her mother was like.

BRIDEGROOM: What does it matter?

MOTHER [*looking at him*]: Son!

BRIDEGROOM: What do you want?

MOTHER: It's true! You're right! When do you want me to ask for her?

BRIDEGROOM [*happily*]: Would Sunday be all right?

MOTHER [*seriously*]: I'll take her those bronze earrings, they're very old. And you buy her –

BRIDEGROOM: You know more –

MOTHER: – buy her some lace stockings. And for yourself, two suits. No, three! You're all I have, now.

BRIDEGROOM: I'm leaving. Tomorrow, I'll go to see her.

MOTHER: Yes. Yes. And let's see if you can make me happy with six grandchildren – or as many as you feel like – since your father had no chance to give me any more children of my own.

BRIDEGROOM: The first boy will be for you.

MOTHER: Yes. But have some girls! I want to embroider, and make lace, and be at peace.

BRIDEGROOM: I'm sure you will love her.

MOTHER: I will love her. [*She starts to kiss him, but draws back.*] Go on. You're too old for kisses. Give them to your wife. [*She pauses. Then, to herself*] When she *is* your wife!

BRIDEGROOM: I'm leaving.

MOTHER: You better hoe the vines over by the little mill. You've been neglecting them.

BRIDEGROOM: Whatever you say.

MOTHER: God go with you.

[*The* BRIDEGROOM *exits. The* MOTHER *remains seated, with her back to the door. A* NEIGHBOUR *wearing a dark dress and a scarf on her head appears at the door.*]

MOTHER: Come in.

NEIGHBOUR: How are you?

MOTHER: Same as always.

NEIGHBOUR: I came down to the store and dropped in to see you. We live so far apart!

MOTHER: It's been twenty years since I've been up to the top of the road.

NEIGHBOUR: You seem well.

MOTHER: You think so?

NEIGHBOUR: Things happen. Two days ago they brought in my neighbour's son – with both his arms cut off by the machine. [*She sits down.*]

MOTHER: Rafael?

NEIGHBOUR: Yes. And there you have him. Many times I think your son and mine are better off where they are – asleep, resting – and not in danger of being left useless.

MOTHER: Don't say that. That's all just talk, but it's no consolation.

NEIGHBOUR: [*She sighs.*]

MOTHER: [*She sighs.*]

[*There is a moment of silence.*]

NEIGHBOUR [*sadly*]: Where is your son?

MOTHER: He went out.

NEIGHBOUR: He finally bought the vineyard!

MOTHER: He was fortunate.

NEIGHBOUR: And now he will get married.

MOTHER [*as if suddenly roused, she draws her chair nearer to that of her* NEIGHBOUR]: Listen!

NEIGHBOUR [*eager for a confidence*]: Yes?

MOTHER: Do you know this girl my son wants to marry?

NEIGHBOUR: A good girl!

MOTHER: Yes, but . . .

NEIGHBOUR: But there is no one who *really* knows her. She lives there alone with her father, so far away – fifteen miles from the nearest house. But she's a good girl, accustomed to being alone.

MOTHER: What about her mother?

NEIGHBOUR: Her mother, I *did* know – she was beautiful! Her face shone like a saint's. But I never liked her. She didn't love her husband.

MOTHER [*harshly*]: The things some people seem to know!

NEIGHBOUR: Pardon me! I didn't mean to offend you, but it's

true. Now whether or not she was a decent woman, no one said. There's been no talk about that. She acted so superior.

MOTHER: Always the same!

NEIGHBOUR: You asked me.

MOTHER: I just wish that no one knew either the one who's alive or the one who's dead. That they were like two thistles that would prick any wagging tongue that touched them.

NEIGHBOUR: You're right. Your son deserves the best.

MOTHER: The best. That's why I take such care of him. . . . I was told the girl was engaged to another man, some time ago.

NEIGHBOUR: She must have been fifteen years old. He got married two years ago – to one of her cousins, as a matter of fact. No one remembers that engagement.

MOTHER: How is it *you* remember?

NEIGHBOUR: You ask me such questions!

MOTHER: We all like to know more about anything that can hurt us. Who was he?

NEIGHBOUR: Leonardo.

MOTHER: Leonardo who?

NEIGHBOUR: Leonardo Felix.

MOTHER [*getting up*]: Felix!

NEIGHBOUR: How could it be Leonardo's fault? He was eight years old when it happened.

MOTHER: That's true. But I just hear – 'Felix'! [*Under her breath*] – and hearing 'Felix' is like having my mouth fill up with slime! [*She spits.*] And I have to spit! I have to spit so I won't kill!

NEIGHBOUR: Control yourself! What do you gain from this?

MOTHER: Nothing. But you do understand.

NEIGHBOUR: Don't stand in the way of your son's happiness. Don't say anything to him. You're getting old. So am I. For you and me, it is time to be silent.

MOTHER: I won't say anything to him.

NEIGHBOUR [*kissing her*]: Nothing.

MOTHER [*calmly*]: Such things . . .

NEIGHBOUR: I'm leaving. My people will be coming in from the
fields soon.
MOTHER: Have you ever seen such a hot day?
NEIGHBOUR: The children who take water out to the reapers are
black from the sun. Goodbye, my friend.
MOTHER: Goodbye. [*The* MOTHER *starts towards the door at the
left. Halfway there, she stops and blesses herself.*]

CURTAIN

ACT ONE

Scene 2

*The room is painted pink, decorated with copper objects and
bunches of everyday flowers. At centre, a table with a tablecloth.
It is morning. Leonardo's* MOTHER-IN-LAW *holds a child in her
arms. She rocks him. The* WIFE *sits in a corner, knitting.*

MOTHER-IN-LAW:
      Sleep, my child, and dream
      About the giant horse
      Who didn't want the water.
      The water, deep and black,
      In among the branches.
      Arriving at the bridge,
      The water stops and sings.
      Who can say, my child,
      What the water holds?
      – With its flowing tail,
      Along its verdant hall.
WIFE [*softly*]:
      Go to sleep, my flower –

The horse does not want water.

MOTHER-IN-LAW:

Go to sleep, my rose –
The horse begins to cry.
His wounded hooves,
His frozen mane,
And in his eyes,
A silver dagger.
They went to the river,
Down to the river!
The blood was flowing
Stronger than water.

WIFE:

Go to sleep, my flower –
The horse does not want water.

MOTHER-IN-LAW:

Go to sleep, my rose –
The horse begins to cry.

WIFE:

He would not touch
The riverside.
His mouth was hot
With silver flies.
He only cried
To the hard hills,
With the dead river
Upon his throat.
The giant horse
Did not want water!
O, sorrow of snow,
The horse of dawn!

MOTHER-IN-LAW:

Stay back! Don't come!
Close the window
With branches of dreams

And dreams of branches.

WIFE:

My child is sleeping.

MOTHER-IN-LAW:

My child is quiet.

WIFE:

O horse, my child
A pillow has.

MOTHER-IN-LAW:

His cradle of steel,

WIFE:

His blanket of linen.

MOTHER-IN-LAW:

Sleep, my child, and dream.

WIFE:

O, the giant horse
Who did not want the water!

MOTHER-IN-LAW:

Don't come! Don't enter!
Go off to the mountain
Through the grey valleys,
The mare awaits.

WIFE [looking]:

My child is sleeping.

MOTHER-IN-LAW:

My child is resting.

WIFE [softly]:

Go to sleep, my flower –
The horse does not want water.

MOTHER-IN-LAW [rising. Very softly]:

Go to sleep, my rose –
The horse begins to cry.

[MOTHER-IN-LAW exits with child. LEONARDO enters.]

LEONARDO: How's the child?

WIFE: He's sleeping.

LEONARDO: He wasn't well yesterday. He cried during the night.

WIFE [*happily*]: Today he's like a dahlia. What about you? Have you been to the blacksmith?

LEONARDO: I just came from there. Would you believe it? For more than two months I've been putting new shoes on that horse, and they keep coming off. He must be tearing them off on the rocks.

WIFE: Could it be you ride him too much?

LEONARDO: No. I hardly use him at all.

WIFE: Yesterday, the neighbours told me they had seen you at the far end of the drylands.

LEONARDO: Who said that?

WIFE: The women who were out gathering capers. It certainly surprised me. Was it you?

LEONARDO: No. What would I be doing out there in that wasteland?

WIFE: That's what I said. But the horse was drowning in sweat.

LEONARDO: Did you see it?

WIFE: No. My mother did.

LEONARDO: Is she with the child?

WIFE: Yes. Would you like some lemonade?

LEONARDO: With very cold water.

WIFE: Why didn't you come home to eat?

LEONARDO: I was with the wheat buyers. They always keep you.

WIFE [*making his drink. She speaks tenderly*]: Are they paying a good price?

LEONARDO: A fair one.

WIFE: I need a dress, and the baby needs a bonnet with bows.

LEONARDO: I'm going in to see him. [*He gets up.*]

WIFE: Be careful – he's asleep.

MOTHER-IN-LAW [*as she enters*]: Who is riding that horse so hard? He's stretched out down there, with his eyes rolling around, as if he'd come from the end of the earth.

LEONARDO [*acidly*]: Me.

MOTHER-IN-LAW: Pardon me! He *is* yours!

WIFE [*timidly*]: He was with the wheat buyers.

MOTHER-IN-LAW: Let him die, for all I care!

[*She sits down. There is a pause.*]

WIFE: Your lemonade – is it cold?

LEONARDO: Yes.

WIFE: Did you know they are asking for my cousin's hand?

LEONARDO: When?

WIFE: Tomorrow. The wedding will be within the month. I suppose they will be coming to invite us.

LEONARDO [*sombrely*]: I don't know.

MOTHER-IN-LAW: I don't think his mother was very happy about
the marriage.

LEONARDO: And perhaps she is right. You have to watch out for her.

WIFE: I don't like you to think badly of a nice girl.

MOTHER-IN-LAW: But he says that because he knows her. Don't
you realize they were seeing each other for three years?

LEONARDO: But I stopped seeing her! [*To his* WIFE] Are you
going to cry now? Stop it! [*He brusquely pulls her hands away
from her face.*] Let's go see the child.

[*They exit, arms around each other. A* GIRL *runs in joyously.*]

GIRL: *Señora!*

MOTHER-IN-LAW: What is it?

GIRL: The bridegroom came to the store, and he's bought the best
of everything!

MOTHER-IN-LAW: Did he come by himself?

GIRL: No, with his mother – tall, dignified. [*She imitates her.*]
And what finery!

MOTHER-IN-LAW: They have money.

GIRL: And they bought some lace stockings. Oh, what stockings!
Women dream of such stockings! Look: a swallow here [*she
points to her ankle*], a boat here [*she points to her calf*], and
here [*she points to her thigh*] – a rose!

MOTHER-IN-LAW: Child!

GIRL: A rose with the seeds and the stem! Oh, and all done in
silk!

MOTHER-IN-LAW: Two wealthy families are going to be joined.

[LEONARDO *and his* WIFE *enter.*]

GIRL: I came to tell you what they're buying.

LEONARDO [*harshly*]: We don't care!

WIFE: Leave her alone.

MOTHER-IN-LAW: Leonardo, don't make so much of it!

GIRL: Please excuse me.

[*She leaves, weeping.*]

MOTHER-IN-LAW: Why do you always have to pick on people?

LEONARDO: I didn't ask for your opinion. [*He sits down.*]

MOTHER-IN-LAW: Very well!

[*There is a pause.*]

WIFE: What is wrong with you? What scheme is boiling up inside your head? Don't leave me this way – not knowing anything –

LEONARDO: Get away!

WIFE: No. I want you to look at me and tell me.

LEONARDO: Leave me alone. [*He gets up.*]

WIFE: Where are you going?

LEONARDO [*bitterly*]: Will you be quiet?

MOTHER-IN-LAW [*resolutely, to her daughter*]: SSSH!

[LEONARDO *exits.*]

The child!

[*She exits, and comes back with the child in her arms. The* WIFE *remains standing, motionless.*]

MOTHER-IN-LAW:

His wounded hooves,
His frozen mane,
And in his eyes,
A silver dagger.
They went to the river,
Down to the river!
The blood was flowing
Stronger than water.

WIFE [*turning slowly, as if in a dream*]:

Go to sleep, my flower –
The horse begins to drink.

14

MOTHER-IN-LAW:
> Go to sleep, my rose –
> The horse begins to cry.

WIFE:
> Sleep, my child, and dream.

MOTHER-IN-LAW:
> O, the giant horse
> Who did not want the water!

WIFE [*dramatically*]:
> Don't come! Don't enter!
> Go off to the mountain.
> O, sorrow of snow,
> The horse of dawn!

MOTHER-IN-LAW [*weeping*]:
> My child is sleeping.

WIFE [*weeping as she slowly moves closer*]:
> My child is resting.

MOTHER-IN-LAW:
> Go to sleep, my flower –
> The horse begins to drink.

WIFE [*weeping, supporting herself on the table*]:
> Go to sleep, my rose –
> The horse begins to cry.

CURTAIN

ACT ONE

Scene 3

Interior of the cave where the BRIDE *lives. Upstage, a cross of large pink flowers. The archway doors have lace curtains tied with pink bows. On the hard white masonry walls are round open fans, blue vases and small mirrors.*

[*The* BRIDEGROOM *and his* MOTHER *enter. The* MOTHER *is dressed in black satin and wears a lace mantilla. The* BRIDE-GROOM *wears a black corduroy suit and a large gold chain.*]

MAID [*affably, full of hypocritical humility*]: Come in. Would you like to sit down? They'll be right here.

[*She exits.* MOTHER *and* BRIDEGROOM *remain seated, as immobile as statues. A long pause.*]

MOTHER: Did you bring the watch?

BRIDEGROOM: Yes. [*He takes it out and looks at it.*]

MOTHER: We have to get back in time. How far away these people live!

BRIDEGROOM: But the land here is good.

MOTHER: Good, but much too lonely. Four hours on the road, and not a house or a tree!

BRIDEGROOM: These are the drylands.

MOTHER: Your father would have covered them with trees.

BRIDEGROOM: Without water?

MOTHER: He would have found it. The three years he was married to me, he planted ten cherry trees . . . [*She thinks back.*] . . . the three walnuts by the mill, one whole vineyard and a plant called Jupiter, with blood-red flowers, but it died. [*There is a pause.*]

BRIDEGROOM: She must be getting dressed.

[*The Bride's* FATHER *enters – an elderly man with shining white hair. His head is inclined. The* MOTHER *and the* BRIDE-GROOM *stand to shake hands with him silently.*]

FATHER: Was it a long journey?

MOTHER: Four hours.

[*They sit down.*]

FATHER: You must have come the long way.

MOTHER: I am too old now to walk along the cliffs by the river.

BRIDEGROOM: She gets dizzy.

[*Pause*]

FATHER: A good hemp harvest.

BRIDEGROOM: Truly good.

FATHER: In my time not even hemp would grow on this land. You had to punish it, even cry over it, before it would provide us with something.

MOTHER: But now, it does. Don't complain – I didn't come to ask you for anything.

FATHER [*smiling*]: You are richer than I am. Your vineyards are worth a fortune. Each young vine, a silver coin! I'm only sorry that our lands – you understand? – are separated. I like everything together. There's one thorn in my heart, and it's that little orchard stuck right in the middle of my property. They won't sell it to me for all the gold in the world.

BRIDEGROOM: It's always that way.

FATHER: If we could take twenty teams of oxen, and bring your vineyards over here, and put them on the hillside – what joy!

MOTHER: What for?

FATHER: What's mine is hers, and what's yours is his, that's why! To see it all together. Because together is beautiful.

BRIDEGROOM: And it would be less work.

MOTHER: When I die, you can sell that place and buy next to this one.

FATHER: Sell! Sell! Bah! Buy, my dear, buy it all! If I had sons, I would have bought this whole hill, as far as the stream. It's not good land, but with muscle you make it good. And since people don't come this way, they don't steal your crops, and you can sleep peacefully.

MOTHER [*after a pause*]: You know why I've come.

FATHER: Yes.

MOTHER: Well?

FATHER: I think it's fine. They have talked it over.

MOTHER: My son has what it takes.

FATHER: My daughter, too.

MOTHER: My son is a good man. He has never known a woman. His reputation is cleaner than a sheet spread out in the sun.

FATHER: What can I tell you about my daughter. She makes bread at three, while the morning star is still shining. She never talks – soft as wool. She embroiders all kinds of embroidery. And she can cut through a rope with her teeth.

MOTHER: God bless your house!

FATHER: May God bless it.

[*The* MAID *enters with two trays – one with wine glasses, the other with sweets.*]

MOTHER [*to* BRIDEGROOM]: When do you want the wedding?

BRIDEGROOM: Next Thursday.

FATHER: The day on which she will be exactly twenty-two years old.

MOTHER: Twenty-two years old. That would be the age of my eldest son, if he were alive. And how alive he'd be – warm and manly as he was! – if men hadn't invented knives!

FATHER: One shouldn't think about that.

MOTHER: Every minute. Look into your own heart.

FATHER: Thursday, then. Isn't that right?

BRIDEGROOM: That's right.

FATHER: The bride and groom and the two of us will go to church in the carriage, since it's so far. And the wedding party in their own carts and on their own horses.

MOTHER: Agreed.

[*The* MAID *crosses the stage.*]

FATHER: Tell her that she can come in now. [*To the* MOTHER] I'll be very pleased if you like her.

[*The* BRIDE *enters, her hands modestly at her sides, and her head lowered.*]

MOTHER: Come closer. Are you happy?

BRIDE: Yes, *Señora.*

FATHER: You shouldn't look so serious. When all is said and done, she's going to be your mother!

BRIDE: I am happy. When I said 'Yes', it was because I wanted to.

MOTHER: Of course. [*Taking her by the chin*] Look at me.

FATHER: She's like my wife, in every way.

MOTHER: Yes? What beautiful eyes! Do you know what being married is, child?

BRIDE: I know.

MOTHER: One man, some children – and a wall six feet thick, to shut out everything else.

BRIDEGROOM: Is anything else needed?

MOTHER: No . . . Just that you all live. Just that! Live!

BRIDE: I will know my duty.

MOTHER: Here are some presents.

BRIDE: Thank you.

FATHER: Shall we have something?

MOTHER: Nothing for me. [*To* BRIDEGROOM] What about you?

BRIDEGROOM: I will.

[*He takes a sweet. The* BRIDE *takes one also.*]

FATHER [*to the* BRIDEGROOM]: Some wine?

MOTHER: He doesn't touch it.

FATHER: That is best.

[*There is a pause. Everyone is standing.*]

BRIDEGROOM [*to the* BRIDE]: I'll come tomorrow.

BRIDE: At what time?

BRIDEGROOM: At five.

BRIDE: I'll be waiting for you.

BRIDEGROOM: When I leave your side, I feel so lost, and I get a lump in my throat.

BRIDE: When you're my husband, you won't feel that way.

BRIDEGROOM: That's what I say.

MOTHER: We must go. The sun does not wait. [*To the* FATHER] Is everything agreed?

FATHER: Agreed.

MOTHER [*to the* MAID]: Goodbye.

MAID: Go with God.

[*The* MOTHER *kisses the* BRIDE, *and they start to leave in silence.*]

MOTHER [*at the door*]: Goodbye, daughter.

[*The* BRIDE *answers with her hand.*]

FATHER: I will go out with you.

[*They leave.*]

MAID: I'm bursting to see the presents!

BRIDE [*harshly*]: Get away!

MAID: Oh, child, show them to me!

BRIDE: I don't want to.

MAID: At least the stockings! They say they're all lace! Please!

BRIDE: I said no!

MAID: For heaven's sake! All right. You're acting like you don't want to get married.

BRIDE [*biting her hand in rage*]: OH!

MAID: Child! My dear! What's the matter with you? Are you sorry you're giving up the life of a queen? Don't think about unpleasant things! Is there any reason? None. Let's look at the presents. [*She takes the box.*]

BRIDE [*seizing her by the wrist*]: Let go!

MAID: Oh, child!

BRIDE: Let go, I said!

MAID: You're stronger than a man!

BRIDE: Haven't I done the work of a man? If only I *were* a man!

MAID: Don't talk like that!

BRIDE: Be quiet, I said! Let's talk about something else.

[*The light begins to fade. A long pause.*]

MAID: Did you hear a horse last night?

BRIDE: At what time?

MAID: At three o'clock.

BRIDE: It must have been a horse that strayed from the herd.

MAID: No, it had a rider.

BRIDE: How do you know that?

MAID: Because I saw him. He was standing under your window. It really surprised me.

BRIDE: Could it have been my fiancé? Sometimes he comes by at that hour.

MAID: No.

BRIDE: Did you see him?

MAID: Yes.

BRIDE: Who was it?

MAID: It was Leonardo.

BRIDE [*loudly*]: That's a lie! A lie! What would he come here for?

MAID: He came.

BRIDE: Shut up! Damn your tongue!

  [*The sound of hoof-beats is heard.*]

MAID [*at the window*]: Look – out there! Was it him?

BRIDE: It was him.

FAST CURTAIN

End of Act One

ACT TWO
Scene 1

The veranda of the BRIDE's *house. The front door is upstage. It is night.*

  [*The* BRIDE *comes out, dressed in ruffled white petticoats covered with lace and embroidered scallops, a white bodice, her arms bare. The* MAID *is dressed as before.*]

MAID: I'll finish combing your hair out here.

BRIDE: It's impossible to stay indoors in this heat!

MAID: It never cools off around here, not even at dawn!

  [*The* BRIDE *sits down in a low chair and looks at herself in a small hand mirror. The* MAID *combs her hair.*]

BRIDE: My mother came from a place where there were many trees, from a fertile land.

MAID: That's why she was so cheerful.

BRIDE: But she wasted away here.

MAID: Fate.

21

BRIDE: Just as we women all waste away. The walls are throwing off heat! Ouch! Don't pull so much!

MAID: I just want to do this wave better. I want it to fall over your forehead.

[*The* BRIDE *looks at herself in the mirror.*]

How beautiful you are! Oh! [*She kisses her with great affection.*]

BRIDE [*severely*]: Keep combing my hair.

MAID [*combing*]: You're so lucky! You're going to hold a man in your arms. You're going to kiss him. You're going to feel his weight!

BRIDE: Be quiet!

MAID: And the best part is when you wake up, and you feel him beside you, and his breath caresses your shoulder, like a nightingale's feather!

BRIDE [*fiercely*]: Will you be quiet!

MAID: But child! A wedding – what is it? A wedding is that, and nothing more! Is it the wedding cake? Is it the bouquets of flowers? No! It's a shining bed, and a man, and a woman!

BRIDE: You're not supposed to talk about it!

MAID: That's something else. But it's such fun!

BRIDE: Or such misery!

MAID: I am going to set the orange blossoms from here to here, so they form a crown on your hair. [*She tries on the orange blossoms.*]

BRIDE [*looking in the mirror*]: Give it to me. [*She takes the orange blossoms, looks at them, and hangs her head dejectedly.*]

MAID: What is this?

BRIDE: Leave me alone.

MAID: This is no time to be sad. [*With spirit*] Give me those flowers!

[*The* BRIDE *throws down the flowers.*]

Child, you're asking for trouble, throwing your crown on the floor! Lift up that head. Don't you want to get married? Say so. You can still change your mind. [*She stands up.*]

BRIDE: They are dark clouds – an ill wind inside me. Who hasn't felt that?

MAID: Do you love him?

BRIDE: I love him.

MAID: Yes, yes. I'm sure.

BRIDE: But this is a very big step.

MAID: You have to take it.

BRIDE: I have already given my promise.

MAID: I am going to put the crown on you.

BRIDE [*sitting down*]: Hurry! They should be arriving soon.

MAID: They've been on the road at least two hours.

BRIDE: How far is it from here to the church?

MAID: Five leagues by way of the stream, but it's twice as far along the road.

[*The* BRIDE *stands; the* MAID *gazes at her with excitement.*]

    The bride is awakening
    On the morning of the wedding!
    The rivers of the world
    Carry your crown!

BRIDE [*smiling*]: Come on!

MAID [*kisses* BRIDE *enthusiastically and dances around her*]:

    Let her awaken
    With the tender blossom,
    Of the laurel in flower!

    Let her awaken
    By the trunk and the tendril
    Of the laurel in flower!

[*There is a loud knocking.*]

BRIDE: Open it! It must be the first guests!

[*The* BRIDE *goes into the house. The* MAID *opens the door.*]

MAID [*surprised*]: You?

LEONARDO: Me. Good morning.

MAID: You're the first one.

LEONARDO: Wasn't I invited?

23

MAID: Yes.

LEONARDO: That's why I came.

MAID: Where's your wife?

LEONARDO: I rode the horse. She's coming along the road.

MAID: Didn't you come across anyone?

LEONARDO: I passed them on the horse.

MAID: You're going to kill that animal with so much hard riding!

LEONARDO: When he dies, he's dead.

[*Pause*]

MAID: Sit down. Nobody's up yet.

LEONARDO: What about the bride?

MAID: I am going to dress her right now.

LEONARDO: The *bride!* She must be happy.

MAID [*changing the subject*]: Where is the child?

LEONARDO: What child?

MAID: Your son.

LEONARDO [*as if from a daze*]: Oh.

MAID: Are they bringing him?

LEONARDO: No.

[*There is a pause. In the distance, voices are singing.*]

VOICES:

The bride is awakening

On the morning of the wedding!

LEONARDO:

The bride is awakening

On the morning of the wedding!

MAID: It's the people. They are still a way off.

LEONARDO [*rising*]: The bride will wear a large crown, won't she? It shouldn't be too large. A smaller one would suit her better. Did the groom bring the orange blossom she's to wear on her breast?

[*The* BRIDE *enters, still in petticoats, wearing the crown of blossoms.*]

BRIDE: He brought it.

MAID: Don't come out here like that!

BRIDE: What does it matter? [*Coldly*] Why do you ask if they brought the orange blossom? Do you have something in mind?

LEONARDO: Nothing. What would I have in mind? [*Approaching her*] You know me – you know I don't. Tell me, what have I ever been to you? Look back, and refresh your memory! Two oxen and a tumbledown hut are almost nothing. That's what hurts.

BRIDE: Why did you come?

LEONARDO: To see your wedding.

BRIDE: Just as I saw yours!

LEONARDO: You tied the knot with your own two hands. They can kill me, but they can't spit on me! And gold may glisten – but sometimes it spits!

BRIDE: That's a lie!

LEONARDO: I don't want to talk about it, because I'm hot-blooded, and I don't want all these hills to hear my shouts.

BRIDE: My shouts would be louder!

MAID: This conversation cannot continue! You must not talk about the past. [*She glances uneasily at the doors.*]

BRIDE: She's right. I shouldn't even be talking to you. But it makes my blood boil to have you come and watch me, and pry into my wedding, and make insinuations about the orange blossom. Get out! And wait for your wife at the door!

LEONARDO: You mean you and I can't talk?

MAID [*furious*]: No! You can't talk!

LEONARDO: Since my wedding, I've thought night and day about who was guilty. And every time I think about it, there is a new guilt that swallows up the old. But there is always guilt.

BRIDE: A man on his horse knows a lot, and he has the power to squeeze the life out of a lonely girl stranded in a desert. But I have pride – that's why I'm getting married! And I will shut myself up with my husband, whom I must love more than anything!

LEONARDO: Pride won't do you any good. [*He comes closer.*]

BRIDE: Don't come near me!

LEONARDO: To keep still when we're on fire is the worst punishment we can inflict on ourselves. What good did it do me to have pride? – and not see you? – and leave you lying awake, night after night? No good at all! It only poured fire over me! Because you may believe that time can heal and walls can hide – but it's not true. It's not true! When things reach deep inside you, nothing can pull them out!

BRIDE [*trembling*]: I can't listen to you! I can't listen to your voice! It's as if I drank a bottle of anisette and fell asleep on a quilt of roses. And it draws me under, and I know I'm drowning, but I follow.

MAID [*seizing* LEONARDO *by the lapels*]: You must leave here right now!

LEONARDO: It's the last time I'll ever talk to her. Don't worry about a thing.

BRIDE: And I know I'm crazy, and I know I'm rotting away with the suffering, and here I am – quietly listening to him, watching him move his arms!

LEONARDO: I can't have peace if I don't tell you these things. *I* got married. Now *you* get married!

MAID: She *is* getting married!

VOICES [*nearer now*]:
        The bride is awakening
        On the morning of the wedding!

BRIDE: The bride is awakening!
        [*She exits, running to her room.*]

MAID: The people are here now. [*To* LEONARDO] Don't come near her again!

LEONARDO: Don't worry.
        [*He exits, stage left. It begins to grow lighter.*]

FIRST GIRL [*entering*]:
        The bride is awakening
        On the morning of the wedding!
        The circle turns, and brings a crown
        To every balcony.

VOICES:
>> The bride is awakening!

MAID [*inspiring their cheers*]:
>> Let her awaken
>> With the tender blossom,
>> Of love in flower!
>>
>> Let her awaken
>> By the trunk and the tendril
>> Of love in flower!

SECOND GIRL [*entering*]:
>> Let her awaken
>> With her long hair flowing,
>> A nightgown of snowflakes,
>> Silver and leather slippers,
>> And jasmine on her forehead.

MAID:
>> O Shepherdess,
>> The moon is rising!

FIRST GIRL:
>> O gallant lover,
>> Leave your hat in the orchard!

FIRST YOUNG MAN [*enters with his hat held high*]:
>> The bride is awakening
>> The guests are arriving
>> To dance at the wedding,
>> With trays of dahlias,
>> And cakes for the wedding.

MAID:
>> The bride is awakening!

SECOND GIRL:
>> The bride is now wearing
>> Her white bridal crown.
>> The bridegroom has pinned it
>> With ribbons of gold.

MAID:

> Under the grapefruit tree
> The bride is unable to sleep.

THIRD GIRL [*entering*]:

> Under the orange tree, the groom
> Offers a tablecloth, a spoon.

[*Three* GUESTS *enter*.]

FIRST YOUNG MAN:

> Awaken, my dove!
> The white dawn unburdens
> Bells in the shade.

GUEST:

> The bride, the white bride –
> Today a maiden,
> Tomorrow a woman.

FIRST GIRL:

> Come down, dusky maiden,
> Trailing your train made of silk.

GUEST:

> Come down, dusky maiden,
> Fresh with the cool morning dew.

FIRST YOUNG MAN:

> Awaken, *Señora*, awaken!
> As orange blossoms rain through the air.

MAID:

> I want to embroider a tree
> Covered with garnet ribbons,
> With words of love on each ribbon,
> And shouts of praise all around!

VOICES:

> The bride is awakening!

FIRST YOUNG MAN:

> On the morning of the wedding!

GUEST:

> On the morning of the wedding,

How enchanting you will be –
Like a flower of the mountains!
Like the wife of a captain!

FATHER [*entering*]:
The wife of a captain
Is taking the bridegroom!
He comes with his oxen
To capture the treasure!

THIRD GIRL:
The bridegroom is golden –
A golden flower.
Wherever he travels
There are flowers in his footsteps.

MAID:
O my happy child!

SECOND YOUNG MAN [*entering*]:
The bride is awakening!

MAID:
O my enchantress!

FIRST GIRL:
The wedding guests are calling
Underneath your window.

SECOND GIRL:
The bride will come out now!

FIRST GIRL:
Come out now! Come out now!

MAID:
They're ringing!
Bells are ringing!

FIRST YOUNG MAN:
She's coming here!
She's coming now!

MAID:
The wedding looms
Like a bull in the ring!

[*The* BRIDE *appears. She wears a turn-of-the-century black dress, with flowers at the hip, a long train covered with pleated gauze and heavy lace, and the crown of orange blossoms in her hair. Guitars play. The* GIRLS *kiss the* BRIDE.]

THIRD GIRL: What perfume did you put in your hair?

BRIDE [*laughing*]: None!

SECOND GIRL [*looking at her dress*]: You won't find material like this anywhere!

FIRST YOUNG MAN: Here's the groom!

BRIDEGROOM [*entering*]: Greetings!

FIRST GIRL [*putting a flower behind his ear*]:

> The groom is gold –
> A golden flower.

SECOND GIRL:

> A peaceful light
> Shines from his eyes.

[*The* BRIDEGROOM *goes to the* BRIDE*'s side.*]

BRIDE: Why did you wear those shoes?

BRIDEGROOM: They're more cheerful than the black ones.

[*Leonardo's* WIFE *enters and kisses the* BRIDE.]

WIFE: Best wishes!

[*The crowd is chattering loudly.*]

LEONARDO [*entering as if to fulfil a duty*]:

> On the morning of your marriage
> We are crowning you with flowers.

WIFE:

> So the meadows may be merry
> With the fragrance of your hair.

MOTHER [*to* FATHER]: Are those people here too?

FATHER: They are family. Today is a day for forgiveness.

MOTHER: I'll put up with them, but I won't forgive them!

BRIDEGROOM: It makes me happy to see you wearing your crown!

BRIDE: Let's leave for the church soon.

BRIDEGROOM: Are you in a hurry?

BRIDE: Yes. I am longing to be your wife. And to be alone with you and to hear no voice but yours.

BRIDEGROOM: That's what I want.

BRIDE: And to see no other eyes but yours. And to have you hold me so tight that even if my dead mother called to me, I couldn't pull myself away from you.

BRIDEGROOM: My arms are strong. I am going to hold you for the next forty years.

BRIDE [*dramatically, taking him by the arm*]: Always!

FATHER: Let's go right away! Get the horses and the carts! The sun has already come up!

MOTHER: But be careful. Let's not have anything go wrong.

[*The large door upstage opens, and they begin to exit.*]

MAID [*weeping*]:

> On leaving your house,
> Maiden so pure,
> Remember: you leave
> Like a star!

FIRST GIRL:

> Clean in body and clothes,
> Leaving your house for the wedding!

SECOND GIRL [*as they leave*]:

> You're leaving your home
> To go to the church.

MAID:

> The breeze is tossing flowers
> Along the sands.

THIRD GIRL:

> Oh, the girl is pure!

MAID:

> The lace of her mantilla
> Is like a shady breeze.

[*They exit. We hear the music of guitars, castanets, and tambourines.* LEONARDO *and his* WIFE *are left alone on the stage.*]

WIFE: Let's go.

LEONARDO: Where?

WIFE: To the church. But you're not going on your horse, you're coming with me.

LEONARDO: In the cart?

WIFE: What other way?

LEONARDO: I am not a man who rides in a cart!

WIFE: And I am not a woman who goes to a wedding without her husband. I can't stand it any more!

LEONARDO: Neither can I.

WIFE: Why do you look at me like that? There's a dagger in each eye!

LEONARDO: Let's go!

WIFE: I don't know what's going on. But I imagine things, and I don't want to. One thing I know: I've already been tossed aside! But I have a son. And another on the way. Let's get started. My mother had the same fate. But I'm not leaving here alone!

[*Voices are heard outside.*]

VOICES:

> On leaving your house
> To go to the church,
> Remember: you leave
> Like a star!

WIFE [*weeping*]:

> Remember: you leave
> Like a star!

That's how I left my house, too! I could taste the whole world in my mouth!

LEONARDO [*rising*]: Let's go!

WIFE: But with me!

LEONARDO: Yes. [*Pause*] Get moving!

[*They exit.*]

VOICES:
>On leaving your house
>To go to the church,
>Remember: you leave
>Like a star!

SLOW CURTAIN

ACT TWO
Scene 2

The exterior of the BRIDE's *cave. Shades of whites, greys, and cool blues. Large prickly pears. Sombre, silvered tones. Views of tablelands the colour of paste, and everything as hard as a landscape on a piece of ceramic folk art. The* MAID *is arranging glasses and trays on a table.*

MAID:
>Turning –
>The wheel was turning,
>And the water was flowing.
>The wedding approaches!
>Let the branches spread open
>And the moon embellish
>Her white veranda!

>[*Loudly*]
Spread the tablecloths!
>[*With pathos*]
>Singing –
>The lovers were singing,
>And the water was flowing.
>The wedding approaches!

33

Let the frost shine and sparkle!
Let the bitter almonds
Be filled with honey!
[*Loudly*]
Bring out the wine!
[*Poetically*]
My lady –
My lady of the land,
See the water flowing!
Your wedding approaches!
You must gather your trousseau
Under the wing of your bridegroom,
Never go from your house –
Because your bridegroom's a dove,
With his whole heart an ember!

The fields await the murmur
Of the blood that has been spilled.
Turning –
The wheel was turning,
And the water was flowing.
Your wedding approaches!
Let the water be glowing!

MOTHER [*entering, with* FATHER]: At last!

FATHER: Are we the first?

MAID: No. Leonardo arrived with his wife a while ago. They must have driven like demons! His wife arrived frightened to death. They got here as quickly as if they had come on horse-back.

FATHER: That man looks for trouble. He has bad blood.

MOTHER: What blood could he have? – That of his whole family, beginning with his great-grandfather who started the killing, and on through the whole evil clan! Men who use knives! People with false smiles!

FATHER: Let's leave it alone!

MAID: How can she leave it alone?

MOTHER: I ache down to the end of my veins! On all their faces I see nothing but the hand that killed what was mine. Do you see me? Don't I seem mad to you? Well, I am mad – from not having shouted everything I needed to. I have a scream in my throat – always there – that I have to choke back and hide under my shawl. But they carry off the dead and you must keep silent. Or people will criticize. [*She takes off her shawl.*]

FATHER: Today is not the day for you to be remembering those things.

MOTHER: When it comes up in conversation, I have to speak. And today more than ever, because today I'm left alone in my house.

FATHER: In hopes of having new company.

MOTHER: That's my dream. Grandchildren.

[*They sit down.*]

FATHER: I want them to have many. This land needs hands that are not hired. We have to keep up a battle – with weeds, thistles and rocks that come from who knows where. And these hands should belong to the owners – hands that will punish and will dominate and will sow the seeds. Many sons are needed.

MOTHER: And some daughters! Boys are like the wind. They are forced to use weapons. Girls never leave the house.

FATHER [*cheerfully*]: I think they'll have some of everything!

MOTHER: My son will have her pregnant in no time. He comes from good stock. His father could have had many sons with me.

FATHER: What I would like is for it all to happen in one day! For them to have two or three grown sons right away!

MOTHER: But it's not like that. It takes so much time. That's why it's so terrible to see your own blood spilled on the ground. A fountain that flows for a minute – and takes years out of our lives! When I got to see my son, he was lying in the middle of the street. I wet my hands with blood, and I licked them with my tongue. Because it was mine! You don't know what that is!

35

I would place the earth soaked with his blood in an urn of crystal and topaz!

FATHER: Now you must wait. My daughter is healthy and your son is strong.

MOTHER: I hope so.

[*They stand up.*]

FATHER: Prepare the trays of wheat!

MAID: They are ready.

WIFE [*entering, with* LEONARDO]: Congratulations!

MOTHER: Thank you.

LEONARDO: Will there be a fiesta?

FATHER: A small one. People can't stay too late.

MAID: They have arrived!

[GUESTS *begin entering in lively groups. The* BRIDE *and* BRIDEGROOM *enter, arm in arm.* LEONARDO *exits.*]

BRIDEGROOM: I've never seen so many people at a wedding!

BRIDE [*gloomily*]: Never.

FATHER: It was magnificent!

MOTHER: Entire families have come!

BRIDEGROOM: People who never left their houses!

MOTHER: Your father sowed the seed, and now you reap the harvest.

BRIDEGROOM: There were cousins of mine that I didn't know any more!

MOTHER: All the people from the coast.

BRIDEGROOM [*laughing*]: They were frightened by the horses!

[*Everyone is talking.*]

MOTHER [*to the* BRIDE]: What are you thinking about?

BRIDE: I'm not thinking about anything.

MOTHER: The wedding vows weigh heavily.

[*Guitars are playing.*]

BRIDE: Like lead!

MOTHER [*strongly*]: But they shouldn't! You should feel as light as a dove.

BRIDE: Are you staying here tonight?

MOTHER: No. There is no one at my house.

BRIDE: You should stay!

FATHER [to MOTHER]: Look at the dance they have started! Dances from far away by the edge of the sea.

[LEONARDO *enters and sits down. His* WIFE *stands behind him, stiffly.*]

MOTHER [*on her way out*]: They are my husband's cousins. As hard as rocks when they dance.

FATHER: I enjoy watching them. What a change for this house!

[*He exits.*]

BRIDEGROOM [to BRIDE]: Did you like the orange blossom?

BRIDE [*staring at him*]: Yes.

BRIDEGROOM: It's all made of wax. It lasts forever. I would have liked you to wear them all over your dress.

BRIDE: There's no need.

[LEONARDO *exits right.*]

FIRST GIRL: Let's go and take off your pins.

BRIDE [to BRIDEGROOM]: I'll be right back.

WIFE: I hope you will be happy with my cousin!

BRIDEGROOM: I'm sure I will be.

WIFE: The two of you here, without ever leaving, raising a family. How I wish I too could live this far away!

BRIDEGROOM: Why don't you buy some land? It's cheap on the hillside, and better for raising children.

WIFE: We don't have any money. And the way things are going . . .

BRIDEGROOM: Your husband is a hard worker.

WIFE: Yes. But he likes to move around too much. He goes from one thing to another. He's very restless.

MAID: Aren't you eating anything? I'm going to wrap up some wine biscuits for your mother – she likes them so much.

BRIDEGROOM: Give her three dozen.

WIFE: No, no! Half a dozen will be enough.

BRIDEGROOM: This is a special day.

WIFE [to MAID]: Where is Leonardo?

MAID: I didn't see him.

BRIDEGROOM: He must be with the others.

WIFE: I will go and see!

[*She leaves.*]

MAID: That is beautiful!

BRIDEGROOM: You're not dancing?

MAID: No one asked me.

[*Two* GIRLS *cross upstage. During this entire scene, people are crossing upstage, animatedly.*]

BRIDEGROOM [*cheerfully*]: That's because they don't know any better. Lively old ladies like you dance better than young ones.

MAID: Are you trying to flatter me, young man? That family of yours! Men among men! When I was a child, I went to your grandfather's wedding. What a figure he cut! It was as if a mountain was getting married!

BRIDEGROOM: I am not as tall.

MAID: But you have the same gleam in your eyes. Where's the child?

BRIDEGROOM: Taking off her crown.

MAID: Ah! Look, for midnight, since you won't be asleep, I put ham and some large glasses of old wine in the lower part of the cupboard. In case you need it.

BRIDEGROOM [*smiling*]: I don't eat at midnight.

MAID: If not you, the bride.

[*She exits.*]

FIRST YOUNG MAN [*entering*]: You have to drink with us!

BRIDEGROOM: I am waiting for the bride.

SECOND YOUNG MAN: Her, you'll have at daybreak!

FIRST YOUNG MAN: That's when it's the most fun!

SECOND YOUNG MAN: Just for a minute!

BRIDEGROOM: Let's go.

[*They exit. There is much chatter. The* BRIDE *enters. The two* GIRLS *run to meet her from the opposite side of the stage.*]

FIRST GIRL: Who did you give the first pin to, to me or to her?

38

BRIDE: I don't remember.

FIRST GIRL: You gave it to me, here!

SECOND GIRL: To me, in front of the altar!

BRIDE [*restless, in a great inner struggle*]: I don't know anything.

FIRST GIRL: I just wish that you'd –

BRIDE [*interrupting*]: And I don't care! I have a lot to think about.

SECOND GIRL: Excuse me.

[LEONARDO *crosses upstage.*]

BRIDE [*seeing* LEONARDO]: And these are anxious moments.

FIRST GIRL: We don't know anything!

BRIDE: You will know when your time comes. This step is one that costs you dearly.

FIRST GIRL: Are you upset with us?

BRIDE: No. Please forgive me.

SECOND GIRL: For what? But either pin means you get married, doesn't it?

BRIDE: Both.

FIRST GIRL: But one of us will get married before the other.

BRIDE: Do you want it so badly?

SECOND GIRL [*shyly*]: Yes.

BRIDE: Why?

FIRST GIRL: Well . . .

[FIRST GIRL *embraces the other. They both run off. The* BRIDEGROOM *enters and very slowly embraces the* BRIDE *from behind.*]

BRIDE [*very startled*]: Get away!

BRIDEGROOM: Do I frighten you?

BRIDE: Oh! It was you?

BRIDEGROOM: Who would it be? [*Pause*] Your father or me.

BRIDE: That's true.

BRIDEGROOM: But your father would have embraced you more gently.

BRIDE [*gloomily*]: Of course.

[*The* BRIDEGROOM *gives her a big hug, in a brusque manner.*]

BRIDEGROOM: Because he is old!

BRIDE [*drily*]: Let me go.

BRIDEGROOM: Why? [*He lets her go.*]

BRIDE: Because . . . people . . . They can see us!

[*The* MAID *crosses upstage again, without looking at the couple.*]

BRIDEGROOM: What of it? It is blessed now!

BRIDE: Yes, but let me go. Later.

BRIDEGROOM: What is wrong? You seem frightened.

BRIDE: Nothing is wrong.

[*Leonardo's* WIFE *enters.*]

Don't go.

WIFE: I don't want to interrupt . . .

BRIDEGROOM: What is it?

WIFE: Did my husband come through here?

BRIDE: No.

WIFE: You see, I can't find him. And his horse isn't in the stable, either.

BRIDEGROOM [*cheerfully*]: He must be out riding.

[*The* WIFE *exits, uneasy. The* MAID *enters.*]

MAID: Aren't you happy with so many good wishes?

BRIDEGROOM: I wish it were already over. The bride is a little tired.

MAID: What is it, child?

BRIDE: There's a sort of pounding in my temples.

MAID: In these hills, a bride must be strong. [*To the* BRIDE-GROOM] You're the only one who can cure her, because she belongs to you.

[*The* MAID *goes off quickly.*]

BRIDEGROOM [*embracing her*]: Let's join the dancing for a while.

[*He kisses her.*]

BRIDE [*in anguish*]: No. I want to lie down a while.

BRIDEGROOM: I'll keep you company.

BRIDE: Never! With all these people here? What would they say? Let me rest a moment.

BRIDEGROOM: Whatever you like. But don't be like this tonight!

BRIDE [*at the door*]: By tonight I will be better.

BRIDEGROOM: That's what I want!

[*The* MOTHER *enters.*]

MOTHER: Son.

BRIDEGROOM: Where have you been?

MOTHER: In all that noise. Are you happy?

BRIDEGROOM: Yes.

MOTHER: Where is your wife?

BRIDEGROOM: She's resting a little. It's a bad day for brides.

MOTHER: A bad day? It's the only good one! For me, it was like coming into an inheritance!

[*The* MAID *enters and goes towards the* BRIDE's *room.*]

It's the ploughing of land, the planting of new trees.

BRIDEGROOM: Are you going to leave?

MOTHER: Yes. I have to be at my house.

BRIDEGROOM: Alone.

MOTHER: Not alone. My head is full of things – and men and struggles.

BRIDEGROOM: But struggles that are no longer struggles.

[*The* MAID *enters quickly. She exits upstage, running.*]

MOTHER: While you live, you struggle.

BRIDEGROOM: I always respect your wishes.

MOTHER: With your wife, try to be affectionate. And if you notice her being distant or shy, caress her in a way that will hurt her a bit. A big hug, a little bite – and then a soft kiss. Not enough to upset her, but enough for her to know you are the man, the master, the one who gives the orders. That's how I learned from your father. And since you don't have him, I must be the one to teach you these strategies.

BRIDEGROOM: I will always do what you say.

FATHER [*entering*]: Where is my daughter?

BRIDEGROOM: She's inside.

[*The* FATHER *goes inside*.]

FIRST GIRL: Come on, bride and groom! We're going to dance The Wheel!

FIRST YOUNG MAN [*to* BRIDEGROOM]: You're going to lead it.

FATHER [*as he comes out*]: She's not here!

BRIDEGROOM: No?

FATHER: She must have gone out on the veranda.

BRIDEGROOM: I'm going to see!

[*He exits. Crowd noises and guitars are heard*.]

FIRST GIRL: They've already started!

[*She exits*.]

BRIDEGROOM [*entering*]: She's not there.

MOTHER [*uneasily*]: No?

FATHER: Where could she have gone?

MAID [*entering*]: The child, where is she?

MOTHER [*gravely*]: We don't know.

[*The* BRIDEGROOM *exits. Three* GUESTS *enter*.]

FATHER [*dramatically*]: But isn't she in the dance?

MAID: She's not in the dance.

FATHER [*energetically*]: There are so many people. Go look!

MAID: I've already looked!

FATHER [*tragically*]: Well, where is she?

BRIDEGROOM [*entering*]: Nothing. She's not anywhere.

MOTHER [*to* FATHER]: What is this? Where is your daughter?

[*Leonardo's* WIFE *enters*.]

WIFE: They ran away! They ran away! She and Leonardo! On the horse! They rode off in each other's arms, like a bolt of lightning!

FATHER: It's not true! My daughter? No!

MOTHER: Your daughter, yes! Born of an evil mother, and him — him, too! But now she is my son's wife!

BRIDEGROOM [*entering*]: Let's go after them! Who has a horse?

MOTHER: Who has a horse? Right now — who has a horse? I'll give you everything I have — my eyes and even my tongue!

VOICE: There's one here!

MOTHER [*to* BRIDEGROOM]: Go! After them!

[*He leaves with two* YOUNG MEN.]

No! Don't go! Those people kill quickly and well! But – yes – run! And I'll follow.

FATHER: It can't be her! Perhaps she has thrown herself into the cistern!

MOTHER: Honourable women throw themselves into the water, the decent ones. Not that one! But now she's my son's wife!

[*Everyone enters.*]

Two sides! There are two sides here! My family and yours! Everyone, leave here! Clean the dust from your shoes! We are going to help my son!

[*The crowd separates into two groups.*]

Because he has his people – his cousins from the sea! And all those who came from the interior! Out of here! Along every road! It has come once again – the hour of blood! Two sides! You with yours and me with mine! After them! After them!

CURTAIN

End of Act Two

ACT THREE

Scene 1

A forest. Night. Great moist tree-trunks. A murky atmosphere. Two violins are playing.

[THREE WOODCUTTERS appear.]

FIRST WOODCUTTER: And have they found them?

SECOND WOODCUTTER: No. But they're searching everywhere.

THIRD WOODCUTTER: They will find them soon.

SECOND WOODCUTTER: Ssshh!

THIRD WOODCUTTER: What?

SECOND WOODCUTTER: They seem to be closing in on every road at once.

FIRST WOODCUTTER: When the moon comes out, they will see them.

SECOND WOODCUTTER: They should leave them alone.

FIRST WOODCUTTER: The world is wide – everyone can live in it.

THIRD WOODCUTTER: But they will kill them.

SECOND WOODCUTTER: You must follow your heart. They did well to run away.

FIRST WOODCUTTER: They had been lying to each other. But in the end, blood was stronger!

THIRD WOODCUTTER: Blood!

FIRST WOODCUTTER: You must follow the course of your blood.

SECOND WOODCUTTER: But blood that is spilled is soaked up by the earth.

FIRST WOODCUTTER: What of it? Better to be dead with no blood than alive with it festering.

THIRD WOODCUTTER: Be quiet!

FIRST WOODCUTTER: What? Do you hear something?

THIRD WOODCUTTER: I hear the crickets, the frogs, the ambush of the night.

FIRST WOODCUTTER: But you don't hear the horse.

THIRD WOODCUTTER: No.

FIRST WOODCUTTER: Now, he must be making love to her.

SECOND WOODCUTTER: Her body was meant for him; his body was meant for her.

THIRD WOODCUTTER: They will track them down and kill them.

FIRST WOODCUTTER: But their blood will have mingled by then! They will be like two empty water jars, like two dry rivers.

SECOND WOODCUTTER: There are many clouds, and it will be easy for the moon not to come out.

THIRD WOODCUTTER: The bridegroom will find them – with the moon or without the moon! I saw him start off – like a raging star! His face, the colour of ashes, revealed the fate of his whole family.

FIRST WOODCUTTER: His family of corpses in the middle of the road!

SECOND WOODCUTTER: That's right.

THIRD WOODCUTTER: Do you think they will manage to break through the circle?

SECOND WOODCUTTER: It would be difficult. There are knives and guns for ten leagues around.

THIRD WOODCUTTER: He's riding a good horse . . .

SECOND WOODCUTTER: But he is carrying a woman!

FIRST WOODCUTTER: We are close now.

SECOND WOODCUTTER: A tree with forty branches. We'll soon cut it down.

THIRD WOODCUTTER: Now the moon is coming out. Let's hurry!

[*The lights grow brighter at stage left.*]

FIRST WOODCUTTER:
> O rising Moon!
> Moon of the giant leaves.

SECOND WOODCUTTER:
> Fill the blood with jasmine!

FIRST WOODCUTTER:
> O lonely Moon!
> Moon of the tender leaves.

SECOND WOODCUTTER:
> Silver on the face of the bride!

THIRD WOODCUTTER:
> O evil Moon!
> Leave the dark bough for their love!

FIRST WOODCUTTER:
> O sombre Moon!
> Leave the dark bough for their love!

[*They exit. The* MOON *appears through the light at stage left. The* MOON *is a young woodcutter with a white face. The stage takes on a vivid blue brilliance.*]

MOON:

I'm a round swan on the river.
I'm the cathedrals' eye.
I'm the false dawn in the treetops.
They will not get away!
Who's hiding there? Who sobs
Beneath the thorns and brambles?
The moon drops down a dagger,
Abandoned in the air –
Ambush of lead that wants to be
The agony of blood.
Let me in! I come, frozen,
Through the walls and windows;
Open your roofs, your breast
Where I can warm myself!
I am cold! My ashes
Of heavy, sleeping metals
Seek the crest of fire
Through the streets and mountains.
But the snow will bear me
Upon its jasper shoulder;
I'll sink beneath the water
Of the frozen ponds.
And so tonight my cheeks
Will fill with crimson blood
And the reeds that huddle
At the wide feet of the wind.
Allow no shade, no shadow –
They will not get away!
I want to enter a breast,
So I can warm myself!
A heart! A heart for me –
Feverish, let it flow
Over the hills of my breast.
Let me in! Oh, let me!

[*To the boughs*]
>   I want no shade. My rays
>   Must enter everywhere:
>   Among the darkened trees,
>   A murmuring of light.
>   So that tonight I'll have
>   Sweet blood upon my cheeks
>   And the reeds that huddle
>   At the wide feet of the wind.
>   Who is hiding? Come out, I say!
>   No! They cannot escape!
>   I'll make the horse shine bright
>   With a feverish diamond light!

[*The* MOON *disappears between the tree-trunks, and the stage lights dim again. A very old woman enters, completely covered in flimsy, dark green garments. She is barefoot. Her face can barely be seen under the folds of cloth. This character does not appear on the cast list.*]

BEGGAR WOMAN:
>   That moon is gone, and they draw near.
>   They'll go no further. The river's whisper
>   And the whispering trunks of trees will drown
>   Their screams, their lacerated screams.
>   Here it will be, and soon. I am so tired!
>   The coffers open, and clean white sheets
>   Are waiting upon the bedroom floor
>   For bodies of men whose throats have been torn.
>   Let no bird wake. And let the breeze
>   Gather their moans in the folds of her skirt
>   And fly with them over the black treetops,
>   Or bury them deep in the softness of mud.
>   [*Impatiently*] That moon, that moon!

[*The* MOON *appears. The intense blue light returns.*]

MOON:
>   Now they are near!

47

Some through the ravine; the other along the river.
I'll shine on the rocks. What do you need?

BEGGAR WOMAN:

Nothing.

MOON:

The wind blows hard, with a double edge.

BEGGAR WOMAN:

Shine on his vest, and open the buttons –
Then the daggers will know their way.

MOON:

Let them be a long time dying.
Let blood hiss softly through my fingers.
See my ashen valleys waken,
Anxious for this trembling fountain!

BEGGAR WOMAN:

We won't let them cross the river. Silence!

MOON:

There they come!

[*The* MOON *exits. The stage lights dim.*]

BEGGAR WOMAN:

Hurry! Lots of light!
Did you hear me? They cannot escape!

[*The* BRIDEGROOM *and the* FIRST YOUNG MAN *enter. The* BEGGAR WOMAN *sits down and conceals herself in her shawl.*]

BRIDEGROOM [*entering*]: This way.

FIRST YOUNG MAN: You won't find them.

BRIDEGROOM [*forcefully*]: Yes, I will find them!

FIRST YOUNG MAN: I think they've taken another path.

BRIDEGROOM: No. A moment ago I heard galloping.

FIRST YOUNG MAN: It must have been another horse.

BRIDEGROOM [*dramatically*]: Listen! There is only one horse in the world – and it's this one! Do you understand? If you follow me, follow me without talking!

FIRST YOUNG MAN: I just wish –

48

BRIDEGROOM: Be quiet! I am sure I'll find them here! See this arm? Well, it is not my arm – it is the arm of my brother and of my father and of everyone in my family who is dead! And it has so much power that it can pull this tree up by the roots, if it wants! And let's hurry, because I feel the teeth of my whole family digging into me – here! In a way that makes it impossible for me to breathe easily.

BEGGAR WOMAN [*whining*]: Ay!

FIRST YOUNG MAN: Did you hear that?

BRIDEGROOM: Go that way, and circle back.

FIRST YOUNG MAN: This is a hunt.

BRIDEGROOM: The greatest there can be!

[*The* YOUNG MAN *exits. The* BRIDEGROOM *goes rapidly towards the left and stumbles upon the* BEGGAR WOMAN: DEATH.]

BEGGAR WOMAN: Ay!

BRIDEGROOM: What do you want?

BEGGAR WOMAN: I am cold!

BRIDEGROOM: Which way are you going?

BEGGAR WOMAN [*still whining, like a beggar*]: That way – far away.

BRIDEGROOM: Where are you coming from?

BEGGAR WOMAN: From there. From very far.

BRIDEGROOM: Did you see a man and a woman race by on horse-back?

BEGGAR WOMAN [*uncovering herself*]: Wait! [*Looks at him*] Beautiful young man! [*She gets up.*] But much more beautiful if you were asleep!

BRIDEGROOM: Tell me! Answer! Did you see them?

BEGGAR WOMAN: Wait! What broad shoulders! Why don't you want to be laid out on them, instead of walking around on the soles of such small feet?

BRIDEGROOM [*shaking her*]: I asked you if you saw them! Have they passed through here?

BEGGAR WOMAN [*forcefully*]: They have not passed! But they are coming down the hill. Don't you hear?

BRIDEGROOM: No.

BEGGAR WOMAN: You don't know the road?

BRIDEGROOM: I will go, whatever it takes!

BEGGAR WOMAN: I will go with you. I know this land.

BRIDEGROOM [*impatiently*]: Then let's go! Which way?

BEGGAR WOMAN [*dramatically*]: Through there!

[*They exit rapidly. Two violins are heard in the distance. They evoke the forest. The* WOODCUTTERS *return, with their axes on their shoulders. They walk slowly between the trunks of the trees.*]

FIRST WOODCUTTER:

Death! Death is coming,
Beneath the giant leaves!

SECOND WOODCUTTER:

Don't start the flow of blood!

FIRST WOODCUTTER:

Death, lonely death,
Beneath the withered leaves.

THIRD WOODCUTTER:

Don't cover the wedding with flowers!

SECOND WOODCUTTER:

Death, mournful death,
Leave a green branch for love!

THIRD WOODCUTTER:

Death, vicious death,
Leave a green branch for love.

[*Each one leaves as he speaks.* LEONARDO *and the* BRIDE *enter.*]

LEONARDO:

Quiet!

BRIDE:

From here, I'll go alone!
Leave! I want you to go back!

LEONARDO:

Quiet, I said!

BRIDE:

>With your teeth,
With your hands – however you can –
Take this metal chain from my neck.
Leave me, let me live forsaken,
There in my house made of earth.
And if you do not want to kill me,
As you would kill the smallest snake,
Then put the barrel of your gun
Into my hands, the hands of a bride!
A song of sorrow – burning! –
Rises up inside my head!
My tongue is pierced with glass.

LEONARDO:

>We've taken the step now. Quiet!
Because they follow us closely,
And I must take you with me.

BRIDE:

>Then it must be by force!

LEONARDO:

>By force? But which of us went first
Back there? Who led me down the stairs?

BRIDE:

>I led the way.

LEONARDO:

>Who untied the horse?

BRIDE:

>I did. I did. It's true!

LEONARDO:

>Whose hands
Put spurs upon my boots?

BRIDE:

>These hands that are yours. They ache
To dig into your flesh
And open each blue vein

To hear your murmuring blood.
I love you! I love you! But leave me!
If I were able to kill you,
I'd wrap you in a shroud
Bordered with violets!
A song of sorrow – burning! –
Rises in my head!

LEONARDO:

My tongue is pierced with glass!
In order to forget,
I put a wall of stone
Between your house and mine.
It's true! Don't you remember?
Seeing you in the distance,
I'd fill my eyes with sand!
But I would take my horse,
And the horse would go to your door.
The silver pins of your wedding
Were making my blood turn black.
The dream was filling my flesh
With bitter, choking weeds!
Because the blame's not mine!
The blame belongs to the earth
And to the smell that comes
From your breasts and from your braids.

BRIDE:

I must be mad! I do not want
To share your bed or food,
But every minute of the day
I long to be with you.
You pull me, and I go along,
And then you push me back.
And helplessly I follow you,
A straw blown on the wind.
I've left a good and honest man,

His family, his house,
In the middle of the wedding,
Still wearing my bridal crown!
But you are the one they will punish,
And I don't want that to be.
Leave me alone! Escape!
No one can help you now.

LEONARDO:

The first wild birds of the morning
Are breaking out of the trees.
And now the night is dying
At the sharp edge of the stone.
Let's find a corner of darkness
Where I will love you always,
And I won't care about people
Or the poison that they spread.

[*He embraces her tightly.*]

BRIDE:

And I will lie at your feet –
Guarding what you dream –
Naked, watching the fields

[*Dramatically*]

As if I were your dog.
Because I am! I look at you:
Your beauty makes me burn!

LEONARDO:

Fire is fed by fire.
The same small flame destroys
Two stalks of wheat at once.
Let's go!

[*He pulls her.*]

BRIDE:

Where are you taking me?

LEONARDO:

Somewhere they cannot go,

>These men who now surround us –
>Where I can look at you!

BRIDE [*sarcastically*]:

>And show me at the country fairs,
>'An Insult to Decent Women'?
>So everyone can stare at me,
>My wedding sheets unfurled
>As if they were my banners?

LEONARDO:

>I would want to leave you, too,
>If I thought like others think!
>But wherever you go, I am going.
>And you, too. Take one step. Only try!
>The moon nails us together.
>My loins are fused to your thighs.

[*This entire scene is violent, filled with great sensuality.*]

BRIDE:

>Listen!

LEONARDO:

>They're coming!

BRIDE:

>Run!
>It's right for me to die
>Here, with my feet in the water
>And thorns around my head.
>And for the leaves to mourn me:
>A lost and fallen maiden!

LEONARDO:

>Quiet! They're here now!

BRIDE:

>Go!

LEONARDO:

>Be still! Don't let them hear us!
>You first. Let's go, I say!

[*The* BRIDE *hesitates.*]

BRIDE:
>>Together!
LEONARDO [*embracing her*]:
>>>As you wish!
>>If they tear us apart, it will be
>>Because I am dead.
BRIDE:
>>>And I am dead!
[*They exit, their arms around each other. The* MOON *emerges, very slowly. The stage takes on an intense blue light. The two violins play. Suddenly their music is cut short by two long, piercing screams. On the second scream, the* BEGGAR WOMAN *appears and stands with her back to the audience. She opens her cloak and remains at centre stage, like a great bird with immense wings. The* MOON *stops moving. The curtain descends on complete silence.*]

CURTAIN

ACT THREE

Scene 2

A room with arches and thick walls. At left and at right, white stairways. Upstage, a very large arch, and a wall of the same colour. Even the floor is shining white. This unadorned room has the monumental feeling of a church. There must not be a single grey, a single shadow – not even one required for perspective. Two GIRLS *dressed in dark blue are unwinding a red* madeja.* *A* LITTLE GIRL *watches.*

* *Madeja*: a skein of wool.

55

FIRST GIRL:

> *Madeja, madeja,*
> What will you make?

SECOND GIRL:

> Jasmine clothing,
> Crystal paper.
> Born at four,
> Dead at ten.
> The woollen thread
> A chain at your feet
> A knot that binds
> Bitter laurel.

LITTLE GIRL [*singing*]:

> Did you go to the wedding?

FIRST GIRL:

> No.

LITTLE GIRL:

> Neither did I!
> What could have happened
> In the budding vineyard?
> What could have happened
> In the olive grove?
> How could it happen
> That no one returned?
> Did you go to the wedding?

SECOND GIRL:

> We told you: no.

LITTLE GIRL [*leaving*]:

> Neither did I!

SECOND GIRL:

> *Madeja, madeja,*
> What will you sing?

FIRST GIRL:

> Wounds of wax,
> The pain of myrtle.

      Sleeping by morning,
      Watching by night.

LITTLE GIRL [*at the door*]:
      The thread is caught
      Upon the flint.
      The azure mountains
      Let it pass.
      It runs and runs,
      And then arrives
      At the stab of the knife,
      The last of the bread.

    [*She exits.*]

SECOND GIRL:
      Madeja, madeja,
      What will you say?

FIRST GIRL:
      The Lover is silent.
      Crimson, the Groom.
      On the mute river bank,
      I saw them laid out.

    [*She pauses, staring at the* madeja.]

LITTLE GIRL [*coming to the door*]:
      The thread runs and runs
      It runs to here.
      Covered with mud,
      I hear them come.
      Lifeless bodies,
      Ivory sheets.

    [*Leonardo's* WIFE *and* MOTHER-IN-LAW *enter, in anguish.*]

FIRST GIRL:
      Are they coming now?

MOTHER-IN-LAW [*sourly*]:
                  We don't know.

SECOND GIRL:
      What can you tell us about the wedding?

FIRST GIRL:
> Tell me!

MOTHER-IN-LAW [*drily*]:
> Nothing.

WIFE:
> I want to return, to know everything.

MOTHER-IN-LAW [*forcefully*]:
> You – go to your house!
> Brave and alone in your house,
> You will grow old and you'll weep.
> Always, the door will be closed.
> Never. Living or dead.
> We'll nail down the windows forever.
> Let the rains come, and night
> Blanket the bitter weeds!

WIFE:
> What could have happened!

MOTHER-IN-LAW:
> No matter.
> Cover your face with a veil.
> Your children are children of yours,
> Nothing else matters to you.
> You must place a cross made of ashes
> On the bed where his pillow has been.
> [*They exit.*]

BEGGAR WOMAN [*at the door*]:
> A piece of bread, girls!

LITTLE GIRL:
> Go away!
> [*The* GIRLS *draw together.*]

BEGGAR WOMAN:
> Why?

LITTLE GIRL:
> Because
> You whine. Go away!

FIRST GIRL:

Child!

BEGGAR WOMAN:

I could have asked you for your eyes!
A cloud of birds follows me. Want one?

LITTLE GIRL:

I want to leave!

SECOND GIRL [*to the* BEGGAR WOMAN]:

Don't pay attention!

FIRST GIRL:

You came along the road by the stream?

BEGGAR WOMAN:

I came that way.

FIRST GIRL [*timidly*]:

Can I ask you –?

BEGGAR WOMAN:

I saw them. They'll soon be here. Two torrents,
Still at last among the boulders.
Two men at the feet of the horse.
Dead in the splendour of the night.

[*Savouring it*]

Dead! Yes, dead!

FIRST GIRL:

Quiet, old woman!

BEGGAR WOMAN:

Their eyes are broken flowers. Their teeth
Are just two handfuls of frozen snow.
They both fell dead. The bride returns
With bloodstains on her skirt and hair.
Covered with blankets, the bodies come,
Come on the shoulders of tall young men.
That's how it was. Nothing more. It was just.
Over the golden flower – filthy sand.

[*She leaves. The* GIRLS *bow their heads, and start to exit, rhythmically.*]

FIRST GIRL:
>> Filthy sand.

SECOND GIRL:
>>>> Over the golden flower.

LITTLE GIRL:
>> Over the golden flower.
>> They bring the dead from the stream.
>> Young and dark, the one.
>> Young and dark, the other.
>> The nightingale of shadow
>> Soars and grieves
>> Over the golden flower!

[*She leaves. The stage is empty. The* MOTHER *enters with the* NEIGHBOUR, *who is weeping.*]

MOTHER: Quiet!

NEIGHBOUR: I can't.

MOTHER: Quiet, I said! [*At the doorway*] Is there no one here? [*She puts her hands to her forehead.*] My son should be answering me! But my son is now an armful of withered flowers. My son is now a dim voice behind the mountains. [*Angrily, to the* NEIGHBOUR] Will you be quiet? I want no weeping in this house. Your tears are tears that come only from your eyes, and mine will come when I am alone – from the soles of my feet, from my roots – and they will burn hotter than blood!

NEIGHBOUR: Come to my house – don't stay here.

MOTHER: Here. Here is where I want to be. And at peace. Now everyone is dead. At midnight, I will sleep – I will sleep at last, without being terrified of guns and knives. Other mothers will be looking out of windows lashed by the rain, to see the faces of their sons. Not me. I will make from my dream a cold ivory dove that will carry camellias of frost over the cemetery. But no! – not the cemetery, not the cemetery! – a bed of earth, a bed that shelters them and rocks them in the sky.

[*A* WOMAN *dressed in black enters, goes to the right, and kneels there.*]

MOTHER [*to the* NEIGHBOUR]: Take your hands from your face. There are terrible days ahead of us. I don't want to see anyone. The earth and me! My tears and me! And these four walls! Oh! Oh! [*She sits down, overcome.*]

NEIGHBOUR: Have pity on yourself.

MOTHER [*pushing her hair back*]: I must be calm. Because the neighbours will be coming, and I don't want them to see how poor I am. How poor! A woman without even one son to touch to her lips!

[*The* BRIDE *enters, without her orange blossom, wearing a black cape.*]

NEIGHBOUR [*looking at the* BRIDE *angrily*]: Where are you going?

BRIDE: I'm coming here.

MOTHER [*to the* NEIGHBOUR]: Who is it?

NEIGHBOUR: Don't you recognize her?

MOTHER: That's why I ask who it is. Because I must not recognize her, so I won't dig my teeth into her neck! You vile serpent! [*She moves threateningly towards the* BRIDE, *then stops. To the* NEIGHBOUR] You see her? She's there, and she's crying, and I – calm – without tearing her eyes out. I don't understand myself. Could it be that I didn't love my son? But what about her honour? Where is her honour? [*She strikes the* BRIDE, *who falls to the floor.*]

NEIGHBOUR: My God! [*She tries to separate them.*]

BRIDE [*to the* NEIGHBOUR]: Let her! I have come so she can kill me and I can be buried with them. [*To the* MOTHER] But not with your hands – with grappling hooks, with a sickle, and with all your might, until it breaks on my bones. Go ahead! But I want you to know I'm unstained. I may be mad, but they can bury me without any man ever having seen himself in the whiteness of my breasts!

MOTHER: Be quiet! Be quiet! What do I care about that?

BRIDE: Because I ran away with another man, I ran away! [*Anguished*] You would have gone, too! I was a woman

61

consumed by fire, covered with open sores inside and out, and your son was a little bit of water from whom I hoped for children, land, health! But the other one was a dark river filled with branches that brought close to me the whisper of its rushes and its murmuring song. And I would go with your son, who was like a little bit of cold water, and the other would send hundreds of birds that blocked my way and left frost on the wounds of this poor, wasted woman, a girl caressed by fire! I didn't want to! Listen to me! I didn't want to! Your son was what I wanted, and I have not deceived him. But the arm of the other dragged me – like the surge of the sea, like a mule butting me with his head – and would have dragged me always, always, always! Even if I were old and all the sons of your son held me by the hair!

[*A neighbour enters.*]

MOTHER: It's not her fault. Nor mine! [*Sarcastically*] Whose is it, then? Loose, weak, indecent woman – who throws off her bridal crown to look for a piece of bed warmed by another woman!

BRIDE: Stop it! Stop it! Take your revenge on me! Here I am! See how soft my neck is? It will be easier than cutting a dahlia from your garden. But that, no! Honourable, as honourable as a newborn child! And strong enough to prove it to you! Light the fire! We'll put our hands in it – you, for your son; me, for my body! You'll take yours out first!

[*Another neighbour comes in.*]

MOTHER: What do I care about your honour? What do I care about your death? What do I care about anything at all? Blessed be the fields of wheat, because my sons lie under them. Blessed be the rain, because it wets the faces of the dead. Blessed be God, who lays us down together to rest.

[*Another neighbour enters.*]

BRIDE: Let me weep with you.

MOTHER: Weep. But at the door.

[LITTLE GIRL *enters; the* BRIDE *remains at the door, the* MOTHER *at the centre of the stage.*]

WIFE [*enters, goes to the left*]:

> He was a handsome horseman
> And now he's a bank of snow.
> He rode through the fairs and mountains
> And into the arms of love.
> And now the moss of night
> Is a crown around his forehead.

MOTHER:

> My child, my son, my sunflower,
> Mirror of the earth.
> Upon your chest, a cross
> Of bitter oleander –
> A sheet to cover you
> With shining, silken strands.
> And water forms a sob
> Between your quiet hands.

WIFE:

> O the four young men
> Who come with weary shoulders!

BRIDE:

> O the fair young men
> Who carry death through the air!

MOTHER:

> Neighbours!

LITTLE GIRL [*at the doorway*]:

> They're bringing them now.

MOTHER:

> It's the same –
> The Cross! The Cross!

WOMEN:

> Sweet nails,
> Sweet Cross,
> Sweet Name –
> Jesus.

MOTHER:

> May the Cross protect the dead and the living!
>
> Neighbours, with a knife,
> With a little knife,
> On a fated day, between two and three o'clock,
> Two men killed each other over love.
> With a knife, with a little knife
> That scarcely fits the hand,
> But penetrates precisely
> Through the astonished flesh
> To stop exactly at the place
> Where, trembling and entangled,
> Lies the dark root of the scream.

BRIDE:

> And this is a knife,
> A little knife
> That scarcely fits the hand,
> Fish without scales or river.
> So on a fated day, between two and three o'clock,
> With this knife
> Two men are left dead,
> With their lips turning yellow.

MOTHER:

> And it scarcely fits the hand,
> But penetrates so coldly
> Through the astonished flesh,
> And stops there – at the place
> Where, trembling and entangled,
> Lies the dark root of the scream.

[*The neighbours, kneeling on the ground, weep.*]

CURTAIN

YERMA

A Tragic Poem in Three Acts and Six Scenes

Cast of Characters

YERMA

JUAN

VICTOR

MARIA

DOLORES

TWO SISTERS-IN-LAW

PAGAN OLD WOMAN

MALE

FEMALE

BOY

SHEPHERD

CHILD

SIX WASHERWOMEN

TWO GIRLS

TWO WOMEN

TWO OLD WOMEN

THREE MEN

SEVEN YOUNG GIRLS

CHILDREN

ACT ONE
Scene 1

When the curtain rises, YERMA *is asleep with a sewing basket at her feet. There is a strange, dreamlike light.*

[*A* SHEPHERD *tiptoes in, staring at* YERMA. *He leads a* CHILD *dressed in white by the hand. The clock strikes. When the* SHEPHERD *exits, the light changes to the cheerfulness of a spring morning.* YERMA *wakes up.*]

VOICE [*singing, offstage*]:
> Nana, Nana, Nana,
> Nana, you will see –
> We will build a little nest,
> And that's where we will be.

YERMA: Juan, do you hear me? Juan!

JUAN [*offstage*]: Coming.

YERMA: It's time.

JUAN [*entering*]: Have the oxen gone by?

YERMA: Yes, they have.

JUAN: See you later. [*He starts to leave.*]

YERMA: Don't you want a glass of milk?

JUAN: What for?

YERMA: You work hard, and you aren't strong enough for so much work.

JUAN: When men stay thin, they get as strong as steel.

YERMA: But not you. When we got married, you were different. Now your face is pale – as if the sun never touched it. I wish you'd go down to the river and swim, and go up on the roof when the rain is pouring down on our house. Twenty-four months we've been married, and you keep growing sadder, thinner – as if you were growing backwards.

JUAN: Have you finished?

YERMA [*standing up*]: Don't take it wrong. If I were sick, I'd want you to take care of me. 'My wife is sick. I'm going to kill this lamb to make a good meat stew.' 'My wife is sick. I'm going to save this chicken fat to rub on her chest.' 'I'm going to take her this sheepskin to wrap around her feet when it's cold.' That's the way I am. That's why I take care of you.

JUAN: And I'm grateful.

YERMA: But you won't let yourself be taken care of.

JUAN: Because there's nothing wrong with me. You're just imagining all these things. I work hard. Every year I will get older.

YERMA: Every year . . . You and I will go on living here every year . . .

JUAN [*smiling*]: Of course. And very peacefully. The work is going well, and we have no children to waste money on.

YERMA: We have no children – Juan!

JUAN: Yes.

YERMA: Do you think I don't love you?

JUAN: You love me.

YERMA: I know girls who trembled and cried before they got into bed with their husbands. Did I cry the first time I went to bed with you? Wasn't I singing as I lifted the linen sheets? Didn't I say to you, 'These sheets smell just like apples!'

JUAN: That's what you said.

YERMA: My mother cried because I didn't mind leaving her. And it was true. No one was ever happier to get married. And yet . . .

JUAN: Quiet!

YERMA: And yet . . .

JUAN: Stop it! It's hard enough for me to be hearing all the time –

YERMA: Don't! Don't keep telling me what people are saying! I can see with my own eyes that it's not true – that when the rain falls on the rocks, they soften and make the wild mustard grow, and people say it's useless. 'That plant is useless.' But I can clearly see its yellow blossoms moving in the breeze.

JUAN: You have to wait!

YERMA: Yes! Wanting! [*Taking the initiative,* YERMA *embraces her husband and kisses him.*]

JUAN: If you need anything, let me know, and I'll bring it. You know I don't like you going out.

YERMA: I never go out.

JUAN: You're better off here.

YERMA: Yes.

JUAN: The streets are for people with nothing to do.

YERMA [*sombrely*]: Of course.

[*Her husband exits and* YERMA *starts towards her sewing, stroking her stomach with her hand. Stretching her arms, she yawns gracefully and sits down to sew.*]

YERMA [*singing*]:

> Where are you coming from, love, my child?
> 'From the ice at the mountain's crest.'
> What do you need, my love, my child?
> 'To be warmed by the cloth of your dress.'

[*She threads her needle.*]

> Let the trees lift their branches up to the sun!
> Let the fountains leap, and the river run!

[*Then, as if speaking to a child*]

> The dog is barking, out in the patio.
> The wind in the trees is singing there.
> The oxen follow the herder lowing,
> And the moon is weaving braids in my hair.
> What do you ask for, child, from so far?

[*She pauses.*]

> 'For the mountains of your white breast.'
> Let the trees lift their branches up to the sun!
> Let the fountains leap, and the river run!

[*She sews.*]

> I tell you, my child – it's true, it's true:
> I am broken and torn for you.
> My womb aches for you –
> An empty cradle, craving you.

When, my child, are you going to come?
[*She pauses.*]
'When your flesh smells like jasmine.'
Let the trees lift their branches up to the sun!
Let the fountains leap, and the river run!
[YERMA *goes on singing.* MARIA *enters through the door with a bundle of clothes.*]

YERMA: Where are you coming from?

MARIA: From the store.

YERMA: From the store, so early?

MARIA: If I had my way, I'd have been waiting at the door when they opened. You'll never guess what I bought!

YERMA: You probably bought coffee for breakfast, sugar, some bread.

MARIA: No! I bought lace, three spools of thread, ribbon and coloured yarn to make tassels. My husband had some money put aside and he himself gave it to me.

YERMA: Are you going to make a blouse?

MARIA: No, it's because – you know?

YERMA: What?

MARIA: Because it's finally happened.
[MARIA *lowers her head.* YERMA *rises and gazes at her in admiration.*]

YERMA: In five months!

MARIA: Yes.

YERMA: Can you tell it's there?

MARIA: Of course.

YERMA [*with curiosity*]: And what are you feeling?

MARIA: I don't know. Queasy.

YERMA: Queasy? [*Holding on to her*] But – when it happened . . .? Tell me! You got carried away.

MARIA: Yes, carried away . . .

YERMA: You must have been singing, yes? I sing. You – tell me –

MARIA: Don't ask me. Have you ever held a live bird tight in your hand?

70

YERMA: Yes.

MARIA: Well, it's the same – but in your blood.

YERMA: How beautiful! [*She stares at her in wonder.*]

MARIA: I'm in a daze. I don't know anything.

YERMA: About what?

MARIA: About what I should do! I'll ask my mother.

YERMA: What for? She's old now and she must have forgotten all that. Don't move around too much, and when you breathe, breathe as softly as if you had a rose between your teeth.

MARIA: Listen, they say that later on he pushes you gently with his little legs.

YERMA: And that's when you love him the most – when at last you say, 'My son!'

MARIA: In the middle of all this, I feel embarrassed.

YERMA: What did your husband say?

MARIA: Nothing.

YERMA: Does he love you very much?

MARIA: He doesn't tell me so, but he comes close to me and his eyes quiver like two green leaves.

YERMA: Did he know when you . . .

MARIA: Yes.

YERMA: How could he tell?

MARIA: I don't know. But on our wedding night he kept saying it, over and over, with his mouth pressed to my cheek – so many times that I feel as if my baby is a fiery dove that he slipped into my ear.

YERMA: You are lucky!

MARIA: But you know more about this than I do.

YERMA: What good does it do me?

MARIA: That's true! Why is that? Of all the girls that got married when you did, you're the only one who . . .

YERMA: That's how it is. Of course, there's still time. It took Elena three years, and in my mother's day it used to take some women much longer. But two years and twenty days, like me, is too long to wait! I don't think it's fair for me to waste away here. Many nights I go out on the patio barefoot, to feel the earth under my feet, and I don't know why. If I go on like this, I'll come to a bad end.

MARIA: Now, look here, child! You are talking like an old woman. Listen to me. You can't complain about these things. My mother's sister had one after fourteen years – and if you could have seen the beauty of that child!

YERMA [*eagerly*]: What did he do?

MARIA: He howled like a young bull, as loud as a thousand cicadas singing at once! And he wet all over us, and pulled on our braids! And when he was four months old, he covered our faces with scratches!

YERMA [*laughing*]: But those things don't hurt!

MARIA: I'll let you know –

YERMA: Bah! I've seen my sister nursing her baby with her breast covered with scratches and it was very painful. But it was good pain – fresh, new, necessary for health.

MARIA: They say children cause a lot of suffering.

YERMA: That's a lie! Mothers who say that are weaklings, complainers! Why do they have them? Having a child is no bouquet of roses! We have to suffer for them to grow up. It must drain half of our blood. But that's good, healthy, beautiful! Every woman has enough blood for four or five children, and if she doesn't have them, it turns to poison, as it will with me.

MARIA: I don't know what's wrong with me.

YERMA: I always heard that the first time is frightening.

MARIA [*timidly*]: We'll see . . . Since you sew so well . . .

YERMA [*taking the bundle*]: Give it to me. I'll cut two little suits for you. What is this?

MARIA: Those are the diapers.

YERMA: Good. [*She sits down.*]

MARIA: Then . . . I'll see you later. [*She approaches* YERMA, *who places both hands lovingly on her belly.*]

YERMA: Don't go running on the cobblestones.

MARIA: Goodbye!

[*She kisses her and goes out.*]

YERMA: Come back soon.

[YERMA *is left as we found her at the beginning. She takes the scissors and starts to cut.* VICTOR *enters.*]

Hello, Victor!

VICTOR [*he is intense and grave*]: Where is Juan?

YERMA: In the fields . . .

VICTOR: What are you making?

YERMA: I'm cutting some diapers.

VICTOR [*smiling*]: Good for you!

YERMA [*laughing*]: I'm going to edge them with lace.

VICTOR: If it's a girl, she'll have your name.

YERMA [*trembling*]: What?

VICTOR: I'm happy for you.

YERMA [*almost choking*]: No – they're not for me! They're for Maria's baby.

VICTOR: Well then, let's see you follow her example. This house needs a child.

YERMA [*in anguish*]: It does!

VICTOR: Then go ahead! Tell your husband to think less about his work. He wants to save money and he will, but who will he leave it to when he dies? I'm going out to the sheep. Tell Juan to pick up the two he bought from me. And as for the other – tell him to dig deeper!

[*He exits, smiling.*]

YERMA [*passionately*]:

That's it! Much deeper!

> I tell you, my child, it's true, it's true!
> I am broken and torn for you!
> My womb aches for you,
> An empty cradle, craving you.
> When, my child, are you going to come?
> 'When your flesh smells like jasmine.'

[YERMA *rises pensively and goes to the spot where* VICTOR

stood. She takes a deep breath as if inhaling mountain air, then goes to the other side of the room as if seeking something, and from there returns to sit down and pick up her sewing again. She begins to sew, but stops and stares at one spot.]

CURTAIN

ACT ONE
Scene 2

In the fields.

[YERMA *enters. She is carrying a basket. The* PAGAN OLD WOMAN *enters.*]

YERMA: Good morning!

PAGAN OLD WOMAN: And a good one to you, pretty miss! Where are you going?

YERMA: I've just taken my husband his lunch. He's working in the olive groves.

PAGAN OLD WOMAN: Have you been married long?

YERMA: Three years.

PAGAN OLD WOMAN: Do you have children?

YERMA: No.

PAGAN OLD WOMAN: Bah! You will have.

YERMA [*eagerly*]: Do you think so?

PAGAN OLD WOMAN: Why not? [*She sits down.*] I just took my husband his lunch, too. He's an old man. He still works. I have nine children, like nine shining suns, but since none of them is a girl, here I am, running from one place to another . . .

YERMA: You live on the other side of the river.

PAGAN OLD WOMAN: Yes, over by the windmills. Who is your family?

YERMA: I'm the daughter of Enrique, the shepherd.

PAGAN OLD WOMAN: Ah! Enrique the shepherd! I knew him! Good people. Get out of bed, work hard, eat some bread, and die. No games, no nothing! Rest and repose – that's for other people. Creatures of silence. I could have married one of your uncles! But no! I have always been a woman with her skirts in the air! I went straight for the slice of melon, the fiesta, the sugar bun! I've often stuck my head out the door at daybreak, thinking I heard the sound of a guitar coming and going – but it was only the breeze! [*She laughs.*] You are going to laugh at me. I've had two husbands and fourteen children. Five died, and in spite of that I'm not sad and I'd like to live a lot longer! That's what I say! Fig trees – how long they last! Houses – how long they last! And only us, confounded women, we are ground to dust by anything at all!

YERMA: I'd like to ask you a question.

PAGAN OLD WOMAN: You would? [*She looks at her.*] I already know what you're going to say. It's not possible to talk about these things. [*She gets up.*]

YERMA [*detaining her*]: Why not? It's given me confidence to hear you speak. For some time I've been wanting to have a talk with an older woman. Because I want to know. Yes! You will tell me . . .

PAGAN OLD WOMAN: What?

YERMA [*lowering her voice*]: What you know. Why am I dry? Am I going to spend my best years feeding birds and hanging starched curtains in my window? No! You must tell me what I have to do, and I'll do whatever it is, even if I have to stick needles in the most sensitive part of my eyes!

PAGAN OLD WOMAN: Me? I don't know anything! I used to lie on my back and begin to sing. The children came like water. Ah! Could anyone say you don't have a beautiful body? Just step out the door, and down the street a horse will whinny! Oh, leave me alone, child! Don't make me talk. I have a lot of ideas I don't want to talk about.

YERMA: Why not? With my husband, I don't talk about anything else.

PAGAN OLD WOMAN: Tell me – do you like your husband?

YERMA: What?

PAGAN OLD WOMAN: Do you love him? Do you want to be with him?

YERMA: I don't know.

PAGAN OLD WOMAN: Don't you tremble when he comes near you? Don't you feel like you're dreaming when he brings his lips close to yours? Tell me.

YERMA: No. I have never felt like that.

PAGAN OLD WOMAN: Never? Not even when you danced?

YERMA [*recalling*]: Perhaps. One time . . . Victor . . .

PAGAN OLD WOMAN: Go on.

YERMA: . . . took me by the waist, and I couldn't say anything to him because I couldn't talk. Another time, this same Victor, fourteen years old – he was a strapping young shepherd – took me in his arms to help me over a ditch, and I began to tremble so hard my teeth rattled! But I've always been shy.

PAGAN OLD WOMAN: What about with your husband . . .?

YERMA: My husband is another matter. My father brought him to me and I accepted him. Happily! That's the simple truth! From the first day we were engaged, I began to think about having children. And I saw myself reflected in his eyes. But very tiny, very manageable – as if I were my own daughter.

PAGAN OLD WOMAN: Just the opposite of me! Perhaps that's why you haven't had a baby yet. Men should be enjoyed, my child! They should undo our braids and give us water to drink from their own mouths. That's what makes the world go round!

YERMA: Yours, but not mine. I have so many dreams, and I'm sure that my son will make those dreams come true. For his sake, I gave myself to my husband, and I keep giving myself to make sure he's on the way – but never for my own pleasure!

PAGAN OLD WOMAN: And the result is, you're empty!

YERMA: No, not empty – I'm filling up with hate! Tell me: is it my fault? Must you look for a man to be a man, nothing more? Then, what are you going to think when he leaves you lying in bed with sad eyes, staring at the ceiling, while he turns over and goes to sleep? Should I lie there thinking about him, or about what can come shining out of my breast? I don't know, but you tell me, I beg you! [*She kneels.*]

PAGAN OLD WOMAN: Oh, what a flower in full bloom! What a beautiful creature you are! Leave me alone! Don't make me talk any more. I don't want to talk to you any more! It's a question of honour and I don't belittle anyone's honour! You'll find out. Anyway, you shouldn't be so childish!

YERMA [*sadly*]: All doors are closed to girls like me, who grow up in the country. Everything is half-said, hushed up, because they say we're not supposed to know about such things. And you, too – you, too – keep silent and walk off with the air of a doctor – knowing everything, but denying it to someone who is dying of thirst.

PAGAN OLD WOMAN: I would talk to another woman who was calmer. Not to you! I'm old, and I know what I'm saying.

YERMA: Then God help me!

PAGAN OLD WOMAN: Not God. I never cared for God. When are you going to realize that he doesn't exist? It's men who have to help you!

YERMA: But why are you telling me this, why?

PAGAN OLD WOMAN [*leaving*]: Though there should be a God, if only a little one, to throw thunderbolts at men whose rotten seed dams up the joys of the fields!

YERMA: I don't understand what you're trying to tell me.

PAGAN OLD WOMAN: Well, *I* understand! Don't feel sad. Keep your hopes up. You're still very young. What do you expect me to do?

[*She leaves. Two* YOUNG WOMEN *appear.*]

FIRST GIRL: Wherever we go, we keep running into people!

YERMA: The men are all out working in the olive groves, and you have to take them something to eat. No one stays home except the old people.

SECOND GIRL: Are you going back to the village?

YERMA: That's where I'm going.

FIRST GIRL: I'm in a big hurry. I left my little boy asleep and there's no one home.

YERMA: Then get going, woman! Children can't be left alone. Are there pigs at your house?

FIRST GIRL: No, but you're right. I'll hurry!

YERMA: Go! That's how things can happen! Surely you left him locked in?

FIRST GIRL: Of course.

YERMA: Yes, but you don't realize what a small child is like. Something that seems so harmless to us could kill him! A tiny needle, a sip of water.

FIRST GIRL: You're right! I'll run. I never really think of such things.

[*She exits.*]

YERMA: Go!

SECOND GIRL: If you had four or five, you wouldn't talk like that.

YERMA: Why not? Even if I had forty!

SECOND GIRL: Anyway, since you and I don't have any, we live more peacefully.

YERMA: Not me.

SECOND GIRL: I do! What a nuisance! On the other hand, my mother does nothing but give me herbs to make me pregnant, and in October we're going to see the Saint – the one who gives babies to any girl who begs eagerly. My mother will beg. Not me!

YERMA: Why did you get married?

SECOND GIRL: Because they married me off. Everybody gets married! If we go on like this, no one will be left single except the children! Well, anyway – the fact is, a girl gets married long before she goes to the church. But the old women are dead set on all of this. I'm nineteen years old and I don't like to cook or clean. Well, now I have to spend the whole day doing things I

78

don't like! And what for? Why is it necessary for my husband to be my husband? We did the same thing when we were engaged that we do now. Old people's foolishness!

YERMA: Hush! Don't say such things!

SECOND GIRL: You'll call me crazy, too! Crazy, crazy! [*She laughs.*] I can tell you the one thing I've learned in life – all the women are stuck in their houses doing things they don't like. You're better off out in the middle of the street! Sometimes I go down to the river, sometimes I climb up and ring the church bells, and sometimes I drink a little anisette.

YERMA: You're a child.

SECOND GIRL: Of course, but I'm not crazy! [*She laughs.*]

YERMA: Doesn't your mother live up at the top of the village?

SECOND GIRL: Yes.

YERMA: In the last house?

SECOND GIRL: Yes.

YERMA: What's her name?

SECOND GIRL: Dolores. Why do you ask?

YERMA: No reason.

SECOND GIRL: You must have some reason.

YERMA: I don't know . . . People say . . .

SECOND GIRL: Whatever . . . Look, I'm going to take my husband his food. [*She laughs.*] Isn't that something? It's too bad I can't say 'my sweetheart', isn't it? [*She laughs.*] Here goes the crazy one!

　　　[*She leaves, laughing happily.*]

　Bye!

VICTOR'S VOICE [*singing*]:
　　　Why are you sleeping alone, shepherd?
　　　Why are you sleeping alone, shepherd?
　　　My blanket is wool.
　　　My blanket is warm.
　　　Why are you sleeping alone, shepherd?

YERMA [*listening*]:
　　　Why are you sleeping alone, shepherd?

79

My blanket is wool.
My blanket is warm.

VICTOR'S VOICE:

Your quilt of dark stone, shepherd.
Your shirt of frost, shepherd.
Grey winter reeds
Your bed at night.
The needles from the oak, shepherd,
Underneath your pillow, shepherd.
And if you hear a woman's voice,
It's the broken voice of water.
      Shepherd, shepherd.
What does the mountain want, shepherd?
There are bitter weeds on the hill.
What child is killing you?
There are sharp thorns on the hill.

[YERMA *starts to go, but meets* VICTOR *as he enters.*]

VICTOR [*cheerfully*]: Where is this beauty going?

YERMA: Was that you singing?

VICTOR: It was.

YERMA: And so well! I never heard you sing before.

VICTOR: No?

YERMA: What a strong voice! Like a gush of water filling your whole mouth.

VICTOR: I'm a happy person.

YERMA: That's true.

VICTOR: As you are sad.

YERMA: I'm not a sad person, but I have enough reason to be.

VICTOR: And your husband is sadder than you are.

YERMA: Yes, he is. That's his nature.

VICTOR: He was always like that.

[*He pauses.* YERMA *sits down.*]

You came to bring his dinner?

YERMA: Yes. [*She looks at him. There is a pause.*] What do you have there? [*Pointing to his face*]

VICTOR: Where?

YERMA [*rising and approaching* VICTOR]: Here – on your cheek.
Like a burn.

VICTOR: It's nothing.

YERMA: To me, it looks like . . . [*There is a pause.*]

VICTOR: It must be the sun.

YERMA: Perhaps.

[*There is a pause. The silence deepens, and, with no outward
sign, an intense struggle between the two begins.*]

YERMA [*trembling*]: Do you hear that?

VICTOR: What?

YERMA: Don't you hear crying?

VICTOR [*listening*]: No.

YERMA: I thought I heard a child crying.

VICTOR: Yes?

YERMA: Close by. Crying as if he were drowning!

VICTOR: There are always lots of children around here who come
to steal fruit.

YERMA: No. It was a baby's voice.

[*There is a pause.*]

VICTOR: I don't hear anything.

YERMA: It must be my imagination.

[*She stares at him.* VICTOR *stares back, then slowly turns
away as if afraid.* JUAN *enters.*]

JUAN: What are you still doing here?

YERMA: Talking.

VICTOR: Stay well!

[*He leaves.*]

JUAN: You should be at home.

YERMA: I stopped for a moment.

JUAN: I don't understand what kept you.

YERMA: I heard the birds singing.

JUAN: Oh, fine! That's how you start people talking!

YERMA [*firmly*]: Juan, what are you thinking?

JUAN: I'm not talking about you. I'm talking about other people.

YERMA: To hell with other people!

JUAN: Don't swear! It's ugly in a woman.

YERMA: How I wish I *were* a woman!

JUAN: Let's stop this conversation. Go home!

　　[*There is a pause.*]

YERMA: Very well. Should I expect you?

JUAN: No. I'll be watering the crops all night. We've had little rain, and it's my turn until sunrise. And I have to keep people from stealing our water. You go to bed and go to sleep!

YERMA [*dramatically*]: I'll go to sleep!

　　[*She leaves.*]

CURTAIN

End of Act One

ACT TWO

Scene 1

The women of the town are doing their washing at the falls in the river, sitting on its various levels. They are singing.

ALL:

　　　　In the icy stream
　　　　I wash your sash.
　　　　Warmer than a jasmine
　　　　Is your laugh.

FIRST WASHERWOMAN: I don't like to gossip.

THIRD WASHERWOMAN: But we all gossip here.

FOURTH WASHERWOMAN: And there's no harm in it.

FIFTH WASHERWOMAN: A woman who wants a good reputation has to earn it.

FOURTH WASHERWOMAN:

　　　　I planted some thyme seeds.

82

See how they grew!
If you want a good name,
Take care what you do!
   [*They laugh.*]

FIFTH WASHERWOMAN: That's what they say!

FIRST WASHERWOMAN: But you never really know.

FOURTH WASHERWOMAN: We do know her husband has brought his two sisters in to live with them.

FIFTH WASHERWOMAN: The old maids?

FOURTH WASHERWOMAN: Yes. They used to have the job of keeping an eye on the church. Now they'll be keeping an eye on their sister-in-law! I wouldn't be able to live with them!

FIRST WASHERWOMAN: Why?

FOURTH WASHERWOMAN: Because they are frightening! They are like those enormous leaves that suddenly sprout up out of graves. They're smeared with wax! Plugged up inside! They probably cook their food in kerosene!

THIRD WASHERWOMAN: Are they already at the house?

FOURTH WASHERWOMAN: Since yesterday. The husband is going out to his fields again.

FIRST WASHERWOMAN: Can I just know what happened?

FIFTH WASHERWOMAN: She spent the night before last sitting on the doorstep, in spite of the cold!

FIRST WASHERWOMAN: But why?

FOURTH WASHERWOMAN: It's hard for her to stay in the house!

FIFTH WASHERWOMAN: These barren women are like that. When they could be making lace or apple preserves, they like to go up on the roof or walk barefoot along some river!

FIRST WASHERWOMAN: Who are you to say such things? She has no children, but that's not her fault!

FOURTH WASHERWOMAN: You have children if you *want* to have them! These spoiled, weak, lazy women were never meant to have wrinkles on their bellies!
   [*They laugh.*]

THIRD WASHERWOMAN: They put on face powder and rouge,

and they wear a sprig of oleander in pursuit of a man who is not their husband!

FIFTH WASHERWOMAN: Nothing could be truer!

FIRST WASHERWOMAN: But have any of you seen her with another man?

FOURTH WASHERWOMAN: We haven't, but other people have!

FIRST WASHERWOMAN: Always other people!

FIFTH WASHERWOMAN: They say it happened on two occasions.

SECOND WASHERWOMAN: And what were they doing?

FOURTH WASHERWOMAN: Talking.

FIRST WASHERWOMAN: Talking is not a sin!

FOURTH WASHERWOMAN: There's something in this world called a 'look'. My mother used to say that. A woman doesn't look at roses the same way she looks at a man's thighs. She 'looks' at him!

FIRST WASHERWOMAN: But at who?

FOURTH WASHERWOMAN: At someone, do you hear? *You* find out. Or do I have to say it louder?

[*Laughter*]

And when she's not looking at him, because she's alone, because he's not right there in front of her, she has his picture in her mind's eye.

FIRST WASHERWOMAN: That's a lie!

[*There is an uproar.*]

FIFTH WASHERWOMAN: What about the husband?

THIRD WASHERWOMAN: The husband acts like he's deaf. He does nothing, like a lizard in the sun.

[*They laugh.*]

FIRST WASHERWOMAN: All this could be straightened out if they had children.

SECOND WASHERWOMAN: All this is what happens to people who don't accept their fate.

FOURTH WASHERWOMAN: Every hour that passes makes that house more like hell! All day long, without ever speaking to each other, she and his sisters whitewash the walls, scour the copper, scrub the windows, polish the floors! And the more that house sparkles, the more like an inferno it becomes!

FIRST WASHERWOMAN: It's his fault, his! If a man can't give his wife children, he'd better keep an eye on her.

FOURTH WASHERWOMAN: It's her fault. She has a tongue that could sharpen knives!

FIRST WASHERWOMAN: What the devil has got into your head to make you talk like that?

FOURTH WASHERWOMAN: Who gave your mouth permission to give me advice?

SECOND WASHERWOMAN: Be quiet!

[Laughter]

FIRST WASHERWOMAN: I'd like to string your muttering tongues on a knitting-needle!

SECOND WASHERWOMAN: Shut up!

FOURTH WASHERWOMAN: And me, the tits of hypocrites!

SECOND WASHERWOMAN: Hush! Don't you see his sisters are coming this way?

[They whisper together. Yerma's two SISTERS-IN-LAW enter. They are wearing mourning. In the silence, they begin to wash their clothes. There is the sound of sheep bells.]

FIRST WASHERWOMAN: Are the shepherds going now?

THIRD WASHERWOMAN: Yes, now all the flocks will be leaving.

FOURTH WASHERWOMAN [inhaling]: I love the smell of sheep.

THIRD WASHERWOMAN: You do?

FOURTH WASHERWOMAN: And why not? The smell of what's yours! Just as I like the smell of the red clay the river brings in the winter.

THIRD WASHERWOMAN: What strange ideas!

FIFTH WASHERWOMAN [looking out]: The flocks are all leaving together.

FOURTH WASHERWOMAN: It's a flood of wool! Sweeping over everything! If the green wheat knew what was coming, how it would tremble!

THIRD WASHERWOMAN: Look at them run! Like enemy troops!

FIRST WASHERWOMAN: Now they're all out. Not one is missing.

FOURTH WASHERWOMAN: Let's see . . . no . . . yes, yes, one is missing!

FIFTH WASHERWOMAN: Which?

FOURTH WASHERWOMAN: Victor's.

[*The two* SISTERS-IN-LAW *sit up and look out.*]

FOURTH WASHERWOMAN [*singing*]:

> In the icy stream
> I wash your sash.
> Warmer than a jasmine
> Is your laugh.
> I want to live
> In the tiny snowdrift
> Of that jasmine.

FIRST WASHERWOMAN:

> Alas, for the wife who is dry!
> Alas, for the wife with breasts of sand!

FIFTH WASHERWOMAN:

> Tell me if your husband
> Still has seed
> To send the water singing
> Through your shift.

FOURTH WASHERWOMAN:

> Your shift is a boat
> Of silver and wind,
> On the edge of the stream.

THIRD WASHERWOMAN:

> I come to the river to wash
> The clothes of my son,
> To teach the crystal waters
> To shine, to run!

SECOND WASHERWOMAN:

> He's coming from the mountain,
> My husband, to eat.

He's bringing me a rosebud,
I will give him three.

FIFTH WASHERWOMAN:

He's coming from the lowland,
My husband, to sup.
He's bringing me hot embers,
Which I will cover up.

FOURTH WASHERWOMAN:

He's coming on the breezes,
My husband, to bed.
My gillyflowers are crimson.
His gillyflower is red.

THIRD WASHERWOMAN:

Join together flower with flower
When summer dries the reaper's blood.

FOURTH WASHERWOMAN:

Open your womb to sleepless birds
When winter trembles at the door.

FIRST WASHERWOMAN:

We must moan on our bed-sheets!

FOURTH WASHERWOMAN:

And we must sing!

FIFTH WASHERWOMAN:

When a man is bringing
The crown and the bread.

FOURTH WASHERWOMAN:

Because our arms will interlace!

FIFTH WASHERWOMAN:

Because the light bursts in our throats!

FOURTH WASHERWOMAN:

Because the green stalk becomes sweet.

FIFTH WASHERWOMAN:

And tents of the wind cover the mountain.

[SIXTH WASHERWOMAN *appears from the top of the falls.*]

SIXTH WASHERWOMAN:
>   So that a child can fuse
>   Crystal shards of dawn.

FOURTH WASHERWOMAN:
>   And our body has
>   Branches of raging coral.

FIFTH WASHERWOMAN:
>   So that there will be oarsmen
>   On the waters of the sea.

FIRST WASHERWOMAN:
>   A little child, a child!

SECOND WASHERWOMAN:
>   And doves open their wings and beaks.

THIRD WASHERWOMAN:
>   A child that sobs, a son!

FOURTH WASHERWOMAN:
>   And the men push forward
>   Like wounded stags.

FIFTH WASHERWOMAN:
>   Joyful, joyful, joyful!
>   The round womb under the nightgown.

SECOND WASHERWOMAN:
>   Joyful, joyful, joyful!
>   The navel, tender chalice of wonder.

FIRST WASHERWOMAN:
>   Alas, for the wife who is dry!
>   Alas, for the wife with breasts of sand!

FOURTH WASHERWOMAN:
>   Let her shine!

FIFTH WASHERWOMAN:
>   Let her run!

FOURTH WASHERWOMAN:
>   Let her shine again!

THIRD WASHERWOMAN:
>   Let her sing!

SECOND WASHERWOMAN:
   Let her hide!
THIRD WASHERWOMAN:
   And let her sing again!
SIXTH WASHERWOMAN:
   The new dawn that my child
   Is wearing on his apron.
ALL [*in chorus*]:
   In the icy stream
   I wash your sash.
   Warmer than a jasmine
   Is your laugh.
   Ha, ha, ha!
   [*They move the pieces of laundry in rhythm, and beat them.*]

CURTAIN

ACT TWO
Scene 2

YERMA's *house. It is growing late.* JUAN *is seated. The two* SISTERS-IN-LAW *are standing.*

JUAN: You say she went out a little while ago?
   [*The* OLDER SISTER-IN-LAW *nods her assent.*]
   She must be at the fountain. But you *know* I don't like her to go out alone. [*There is a pause.*] You can set the table.
   [*The* YOUNGER SISTER-IN-LAW *exits.*]
   I really earn the bread I eat! [*To the* SISTER-IN-LAW] Yesterday I had a hard day. I was pruning the apple trees and by the end of the afternoon I began to think – why am I working so hard if I can't even put one apple in my mouth? I'm fed up! [*He passes*

89

his hand over his face. There is a pause.] She hasn't come. One of you should always go with her! That's why you're here, eating at my table and drinking my wine! My work is in the fields, but my honour is here. And my honour is yours, as well. [*The* SISTER-IN-LAW *bows her head.*] Don't take me wrong.

[YERMA *enters carrying two pitchers. She stops in the doorway.*]

Have you been to the fountain?

YERMA: Yes, so we could have fresh water with our dinner.

[*The other* SISTER-IN-LAW *exits.*]

How are things in the fields?

[YERMA *sets down the pitchers. There is a pause.*]

JUAN: I spent yesterday pruning trees.

YERMA: Will you be staying?

JUAN: I have to take care of the flock. If you have sheep, you know, it's your duty.

YERMA: I know it very well. Don't say it again!

JUAN: Every man has his work.

YERMA: And every woman, hers! I'm not asking you to stay. I have everything I need here. Your sisters watch over me very well. Here, I eat fresh bread and cheese and roast lamb, and in the mountains your sheep graze on grass washed with dew. I think you can live in peace.

JUAN: To live in peace, you have to be at peace!

YERMA: And you are not.

JUAN: I am not.

YERMA: Change your way of thinking!

JUAN: Don't you know the way I think? The sheep in the pens, and the women in their houses. You're out too much! Haven't you always heard me say that?

YERMA: You're right! The women in their houses. If the houses are not tombs! If chairs get broken, and linen sheets wear out from being used! But not here! Every night, when I get into bed, the bed seems to be newer, shinier, as if it had just been brought from the city.

JUAN: You yourself admit that I have reason to complain! That I have reason to be on my guard.

YERMA: On your guard against what? I don't do anything to hurt you! I am always submissive to you, and whatever I suffer, I keep to myself. And each day that goes by will be worse. Let's stop talking! I'll carry my cross the best I can, just don't ask me any questions! If I could suddenly become old, with a mouth like a crushed flower, then I could smile at you and share life with you. Now – now, leave me to my agony!

JUAN: You're talking in a way I don't understand. I deprive you of nothing! I send to nearby towns for things you like. I have my faults, but I want to have peace and quiet with you. I want to be able to sleep when I'm away and to know that you're sleeping, too!

YERMA: But I don't sleep, I can't sleep!

JUAN: Is there something you need? Tell me. Answer me!

YERMA [*meaningfully, staring at her husband*]: Yes, I need something!

[*There is a pause.*]

JUAN: Always the same! It's been more than five years now! I've almost forgotten about it.

YERMA: But I'm not you! Men have another life – their flocks, their orchards, their conversations! Women only have their children and caring for their children.

JUAN: Everyone is not the same. Why don't you take in one of your brother's children? I wouldn't be against it.

YERMA: I don't want to take care of other people's children! I think my arms would freeze, just holding them!

JUAN: Always brooding about this is driving you crazy; you never think about the things you should, and you insist on beating your head against a rock!

YERMA: A rock that is shameful – because it *is* a rock, when it should be a basket of flowers and sweet water!

JUAN: Being around you only makes me restless and uneasy. When there's no other choice, you should resign yourself.

YERMA: I came to this house so I wouldn't have to resign myself! When I'm in my coffin with my hands tied together and a cloth wrapped around my head to keep my mouth from falling open – that's when I'll resign myself!

JUAN: Then what do you want to do?

YERMA: I want to drink water and there's no glass and no water! I want to walk up the hill, and I have no feet! I want to embroider my petticoats, and I can't find the thread!

JUAN: The truth is you're not a real woman, and you're trying to destroy a man who has no choice!

YERMA: I don't know who I am. Let go of me, let me unburden myself! I have never failed you!

JUAN: I don't like people pointing at me! That's why I want to see that door locked and everyone in her own house!

[FIRST SISTER-IN-LAW *enters slowly and goes towards a cupboard.*]

YERMA: Talking to people is not a sin!

JUAN: But it can seem like one!

[*The* SECOND SISTER-IN-LAW *enters and goes to the pitchers, from which she fills a water jug.*]

JUAN [*lowering his voice*]: I don't have the strength for all this. When people start a conversation, close your mouth and remember you're a married woman!

YERMA [*amazed*]: Married!

JUAN: And that families have their honour, and honour is a burden all of them must bear!

[*The* SECOND SISTER-IN-LAW *slowly exits with the water jug.*]

But inside our bloodstream, it's dark and weak.

[*The* FIRST SISTER-IN-LAW *exits with a tray. Her gait is almost processional. There is a pause.*]

Forgive me.

[YERMA *looks at her husband. He raises his head and is held by her gaze.*]

Though the way you are looking at me, I shouldn't say 'Forgive me'. I should force you, lock you up, because that's what a husband is for!

[*The two* SISTERS-IN-LAW *appear at the door.*]

YERMA: I beg you not to talk! Let the matter rest!

[*There is a pause.*]

JUAN: Let's eat!

[*The two* SISTERS-IN-LAW *exit.*]

JUAN: Did you hear me?

YERMA [*sweetly*]: You eat with your sisters. I'm not hungry yet.

JUAN: As you wish.

[*He exits.*]

YERMA [*as if in a dream*]:

O what a pasture of pain!
O the gate barred against beauty!
I crave to carry a child, but the breeze
Offers dahlias made of the dreaming moon.
Deep in my flesh I have two warm springs,
Two throbbing fountain-heads of milk –
The pulsing hoof-beats of a horse,
Which agitate the branches of my anguish.
O blind breasts under my clothing!
O doves without eyes, doves without whiteness!
The stinging pain of imprisoned blood
Nails hornets to the nape of my neck!
But surely you'll come, my love, my son!
As the sea gives salt, and the earth bears grain,
Our womb will swell with a tender child,
Like a cloud which brings the sweet, fresh rain.

[*Looking towards the door*] Maria, why do you pass my house in such a hurry?

MARIA [*entering with a baby in her arms*]: When I have the baby with me, I do – since you always cry!

YERMA: That's true. [*She takes the baby and sits down.*]

MARIA: It makes me sad that you are envious.

YERMA: I'm not envious – I'm deprived.

MARIA: Don't complain.

YERMA: How can I keep from complaining, when I see you and the other women in full bloom, and I see myself useless in the middle of so much beauty?

MARIA: But you have other things. If you'd listen to me, you could be happy.

YERMA: A country girl who doesn't bear children is as useless as a handful of thorns – even sinful! And so, I'm part of the refuse discarded by God's hand!

[MARIA *reaches for the child*.]

Take him, he's happier with you! I suppose I don't have a mother's hands!

MARIA: Why do you say that?

YERMA [*getting up*]: Because I'm sick of it! Because I'm sick of having them and not being able to use them for the right thing. Because I'm hurt – hurt and completely degraded – watching how the wheat springs up, how the fountains never cease giving water, and how the sheep give birth to hundreds of lambs, and the dogs, and how it seems as if the whole countryside rises up to show me its young offspring, drowsily nursing, while I feel the blows of a hammer, here, where my baby's mouth should be!

MARIA: I don't like what you're saying!

YERMA: You women who have children, you can't understand those of us who don't! You stay fresh, ignorant – like people who swim in sweet water with no idea what thirst is.

MARIA: I don't want to tell you what I always tell you.

YERMA: Each time I have more need, and less hope!

MARIA: How awful!

YERMA: I'll end up believing that I'm my own son. I often go down to feed the oxen – which I never used to do, because women don't – and when I walk through the dark shed, my footsteps sound to me like those of a man.

MARIA: We are all here for a reason.

YERMA: In spite of everything, he goes on wanting me. Now you see how I live!

MARIA: What about his sisters?

YERMA: I'll be dead and buried before I'll ever speak to them!

MARIA: What about your husband?

YERMA: The three of them are against me.

MARIA: What do they think?

YERMA: They imagine things. Like people with a guilty conscience. They think I could want another man, and don't realize that even if I did, in my family, honour comes first! They are stones in my path! But they don't know that if I want to, I can become a torrent of water and sweep them away!

[A SISTER-IN-LAW *enters and then exits, carrying a loaf of bread.*]

MARIA: Anyway, I think your husband still loves you.

YERMA: My husband gives me bread and board.

MARIA: What a hard time you're having, what a hard time! But remember the wounds of Our Lord.

[*They are at the doorway.*]

YERMA [*looking at the child*]: He's awake now.

MARIA: In a little while he'll start to sing!

YERMA: The same eyes as you, you know that? Have you seen them? [*Weeping*] He has the same eyes that you have.

[YERMA *gently pushes* MARIA, *who leaves in silence.* YERMA *goes towards the door through which her husband left. The* SECOND YOUNG WOMAN *appears.*]

SECOND YOUNG WOMAN: Psst!

YERMA [*turning*]: What?

SECOND YOUNG WOMAN: I waited for her to leave. My mother is expecting you.

YERMA: Is she alone?

SECOND YOUNG WOMAN: Two neighbours are with her.

YERMA: Tell them to wait a bit.

SECOND YOUNG WOMAN: But are you going? Aren't you afraid?

YERMA: I am going.

SECOND YOUNG WOMAN: Whatever you say!

YERMA: Have them wait for me, even if it's late!

[VICTOR *enters*.]

VICTOR: Is Juan at home?

YERMA: Yes.

SECOND YOUNG WOMAN [*conspiring*]: As I was saying, I'll bring the blouse later.

YERMA: Whenever you like.

[*The* YOUNG WOMAN *leaves*.]

Sit down.

VICTOR: I'm fine this way.

YERMA [*calling*]: Juan!

VICTOR: I've come to say goodbye.

[YERMA *trembles slightly, but recovers her composure*.]

YERMA: Are you going to live with your brothers?

VICTOR: That's what my father wants.

YERMA: He must be old now.

VICTOR: Yes, very old.

[*There is a pause*.]

YERMA: A change of scenery will do you good.

VICTOR: All scenery is the same.

YERMA: No. I would go very far away.

VICTOR: It's all the same. The same sheep have the same wool.

YERMA: For men, yes; but women are another matter. I never heard a man who was eating say, 'How good these apples are!' You go on your way without noticing the nice things. As for me, I can say I have hated the water from these wells!

VICTOR: It could be.

[*The stage is in soft shadow*.]

YERMA: Victor.

VICTOR: Yes.

YERMA: Why are you leaving? Everybody here likes you.

VICTOR: I've behaved.

[*There is a pause*.]

YERMA: You've behaved. One time, when you were a strong young shepherd, you carried me in your arms, don't you remember? You never know what's going to happen.

VICTOR: Everything changes.

YERMA: Some things don't change! There are things locked up behind the walls that can never change because nobody hears them!

VICTOR: That's how it is.

[*The* SECOND SISTER-IN-LAW *appears and goes slowly towards the door, where she stands still, illuminated by the last light of afternoon.*]

YERMA: But if they suddenly exploded, they would shake the world!

VICTOR: Nothing would be gained. The water in its channel, the flock in the fold, the moon in the sky, and a man with his plough!

YERMA: What a terrible shame not to be able to learn from the teachings of the old people!

[*There is the long, melancholy sound made by a shepherd blowing on a conch shell.*]

VICTOR: The flocks.

JUAN [*entering*]: Are you on your way now?

VICTOR: I want to get through the mountain pass before daybreak.

JUAN: Do I owe you anything?

VICTOR: No. You paid me well.

JUAN [*to* YERMA]: I bought his flocks.

YERMA: Yes?

VICTOR [*to* YERMA]: They're yours.

YERMA: I didn't know.

JUAN [*with satisfaction*]: It's true!

VICTOR: Your husband should see his fortune made!

YERMA: He who labours gets the fruit.

[*The* SISTER-IN-LAW *who is at the door goes inside.*]

JUAN: We don't have enough room for so many sheep!

YERMA [*sombrely*]: There's so much land!

[*There is a pause.*]

JUAN: We'll go together as far as the stream.

VICTOR: I wish great happiness for this house!

[*He shakes* YERMA'*s hand.*]

YERMA: May God hear you. Stay well!

[VICTOR *starts to leave but, after an imperceptible movement by* YERMA, *he turns back.*]

VICTOR: Did you say something?

YERMA [*dramatically*]: I said 'Stay well!'

VICTOR: Thank you.

[*They leave.* YERMA *is left in anguish, looking at the hand which* VICTOR *shook. Then she quickly crosses to the left, and picks up a shawl.*]

SECOND YOUNG WOMAN [*entering*]: Let's go!

[*In silence, she covers* YERMA'*s head.*]

YERMA: Let's go!

[*They leave, stealthily. The stage is almost dark. The* FIRST SISTER-IN-LAW *enters with an oil-lamp which casts the only light on the stage. She goes to the edge of the stage looking for* YERMA. *The shepherds' conch shells sound.*]

FIRST SISTER-IN-LAW [*softly*]: Yerma!

[*The* SECOND SISTER-IN-LAW *enters. They look at each other and then move towards the door.*]

SECOND SISTER-IN-LAW [*louder*]: Yerma!

FIRST SISTER-IN-LAW [*as she goes out the door, in an imperious voice*]: Yerma!

[*We hear shepherds' horns and their dogs. The stage is extremely dark.*]

CURTAIN

End of Act Two

ACT THREE

Scene 1

The house of DOLORES, *the conjuror. Day is breaking.*

[YERMA *enters with* DOLORES *and* TWO OLD WOMEN.]

DOLORES: You were very brave!

FIRST OLD WOMAN: There's no force in the world like that of desire.

SECOND OLD WOMAN: But the cemetery was so dark!

DOLORES: I've said those prayers in the cemetery many times with women eager to have babies, and they were all afraid! All but you!

YERMA: I came for the result. I don't believe you're a deceitful woman.

DOLORES: I'm not! Let my tongue crawl with ants, like the mouths of the dead, if I have ever told a lie! The last time, I said the prayer with a beggar woman who'd been dry much longer than you, and her womb sweetened so beautifully she had two babies, down there by the river, because she didn't have time to get to the village, and she herself brought them in swaddling clothes for me to tend to.

YERMA: And she was able to walk here from the river?

DOLORES: She got here. With her shoes and her petticoats soaked with blood – but with her face shining!

YERMA: And nothing happened to her?

DOLORES: What could happen? God is God.

YERMA: Of course, God is God! Nothing could happen to her. Just pick up the babies and wash them in fresh water! Animals lick them, don't they? With my own child, that wouldn't disgust me. I have the notion that women who have just given birth are glowing inside, and that their babies sleep on top of them for hours and hours, listening to the stream of warm milk that goes on filling their breasts so they can suckle, so they can play

99

until they don't want any more, until they pull their heads away. 'Just a little bit more, my child . . .' And their faces and chests are covered with white drops!

DOLORES: Now you will have a child. I can assure you.

YERMA: I will have one because I must! Or I don't understand the world. Sometimes, when I'm sure that never, never . . . a wave of fire sweeps up from my feet, and makes everything seem empty. And men walking along the street, and bulls and stones, seem to me like things made of cotton. And I ask myself: 'What are they there for?'

FIRST OLD WOMAN: It's all right for a married woman to want children, but if she doesn't have them, why this anxiety for them? What's important in this world is to just drift along with the years. I'm not criticizing you. You saw how I helped with the praying. But what lush land do you hope to leave your son, or what good fortune, or what silver throne?

YERMA: I don't think about tomorrow, I think about today! You're old, and now you see everything like a book you've read before. I think I am thirsty, but I have no freedom! I want to hold my child in my arms so I can sleep peacefully! And listen carefully, and don't be frightened by what I say: even if I knew that one day my son was going to torture me, and hate me, and drag me through the streets by the hair, I would still rejoice at his birth! It's much better to cry over a man who is alive and stabs you with a knife, than to cry over this phantom sitting on my heart, year after year!

FIRST OLD WOMAN: You're too young to listen to advice! But while you're waiting for the Grace of God, you should find shelter in your husband's love.

YERMA: Ay! You've put your finger into the deepest wound in my flesh!

DOLORES: Your husband is good.

YERMA [she gets up]: He is good. He is good! What of it? I wish he were bad! But no! He takes his sheep along their paths and counts his money at night. When he takes me, he is doing his duty, but his body feels as cold as a corpse! I have always been disgusted by hot-blooded women, but at that moment I would like to be a mountain of fire!

DOLORES: Yerma!

YERMA: I'm not an unfaithful wife, but I know that children are conceived by a man and a woman. Oh, if only I could have them all by myself!

DOLORES: Think how your husband suffers, too.

YERMA: He doesn't suffer! The fact is, he doesn't want children.

FIRST OLD WOMAN: Don't say that!

YERMA: I can see it in his eyes, and since he doesn't want them, he doesn't give them to me. I don't love him, I don't love him, and yet he's my only salvation! For honour and for family! My only salvation!

FIRST OLD WOMAN [*fearfully*]: Soon it will be dawn! You should go home.

DOLORES: Before you know it, the flocks will be coming out, and it's not good for you to be seen alone!

YERMA: I needed to get this off my chest. How many times do I repeat the prayers?

DOLORES: The prayer of the laurel twice, and at noon the prayer of Santa Ana. When you feel you're pregnant, bring me the bushel of wheat you promised me.

FIRST OLD WOMAN: Now it's beginning to grow light on top of the hills. Go!

DOLORES: Any minute, people will be opening up their doors, so you'd better go around by the water ditch.

YERMA [*disheartened*]: I don't know why I came.

DOLORES: Are you sorry?

YERMA: No!

DOLORES [*upset*]: If you're afraid, I'll go with you as far as the corner.

FIRST OLD WOMAN [*uneasily*]: It will be daylight by the time you get to your door.

[*Voices are heard.*]

DOLORES: Be quiet!

[*They listen.*]

FIRST OLD WOMAN: It's no one. God go with you!

[YERMA *goes towards the door, but at that moment a knock is heard. The three women stop still.*]

DOLORES: Who is it?

JUAN'S VOICE: It's me!

YERMA: Open it!

[DOLORES *is unsure.*]

Are you going to open it or not?

[*Murmuring is heard.* JUAN *and the* SISTERS-IN-LAW *appear.*]

SECOND SISTER-IN-LAW: Here she is!

YERMA: Here I am!

JUAN: What are you doing in this place? If I could shout, I would rouse the whole village so they could see what's become of my family honour! But I have to choke it all back and keep quiet, because you are my wife.

YERMA: If I could, I would shout, too – so even the dead would rise up and see that I am cloaked in purity!

JUAN: No, not that! I can put up with anything but that! You deceive me, you confuse me, but I'm only a man who works the land and I can't compete with your cleverness!

DOLORES: Juan!

JUAN: Not a word out of any of you!

DOLORES [*firmly*]: Your wife has done nothing wrong.

JUAN: She's been doing it since the very day of our wedding. Looking daggers at me, spending the nights on watch, lying at my side with her eyes open, and filling my pillows with her unhappy sighs!

YERMA: Shut your mouth!

JUAN: And I can't stand any more! You'd have to be made of bronze to put up with a woman at your side who wants to jab her fingers into your heart and goes out of her house at night – looking for what? Tell me! Looking for what? The streets are full of young studs. You don't go out on the streets to pick flowers!

YERMA: I won't let you say one more word! Not one more! You and your family think you're the only people who care about honour, and you don't know that my family has never had anything to hide. Come here! Come close to me and smell my clothing; come close! Let's see where you can find a smell that's not yours, that's not from your body! Stand me naked in the middle of the plaza and spit on me! Do what you like with me, since I'm your wife, but take care you don't put another man's name on my breast!

JUAN: It's not me who puts it there – you put it there with your behaviour, and the town is beginning to talk! Beginning to talk! When I join a group of people, they all grow quiet. When I go to weigh the flour, they all grow quiet. And even at night, when I wake up in the fields, it seems as if the branches of the trees grow quiet, too!

YERMA: Those evil winds that knock the wheat down – I don't know why they start. See for yourself if the wheat is good!

JUAN: Nor do I know what a woman is looking for, out of her house at all hours!

YERMA [in an outburst, embracing her husband]: I'm looking for you! I'm looking for you! It's you I look for, day and night, without finding any shade where I can rest! It's your blood and your help I want!

JUAN: Get away!

YERMA: Don't push me away – want with me!

JUAN: Stop it!

YERMA: See how alone I am! Like the moon trying to find herself in the sky. Look at me! [She looks at him.]

JUAN [looking at her, and brusquely pushing her away]: Leave me alone, once and for all!

DOLORES: Juan!

[YERMA falls to the ground.]

YERMA [loudly]: When I went out to pick my carnations I ran

into the wall. [*She wails.*] That is the wall where I have to smash my head to bits!

JUAN: Be quiet! Let's go!

DOLORES: My God!

YERMA [*screaming*]: God damn my father for giving me his blood – the blood of the father of a hundred sons! God damn my blood that pounds on the walls looking for them!

JUAN: Be quiet, I said!

DOLORES: People are coming! Talk softly!

YERMA: I don't care! At least let my voice be free, now that I'm falling into the darkest part of the pit! [*She gets up.*] Let my body send out·just one beautiful thing, and let it fill the air.

[*Voices are heard.*]

DOLORES: They're going to pass by here.

JUAN: Silence!

YERMA: Of course. Of course. Silence. Don't worry.

JUAN: Let's go! Quickly!

YERMA: All right! All right! And there's no use wringing my hands. Wanting for something in your mind is one thing –

JUAN: Be quiet!

YERMA [*in a low voice*]: Wanting something in your head is one thing, but it's something else when your body – damn the body! – won't respond. This is my fate and I'm not going to fight against the tide. That's it! Let my lips be sealed!

[*She leaves.*]

FAST CURTAIN

ACT THREE

Scene 2

On the grounds of a shrine, high in the mountains. Down stage, the wheels of a cart and some blankets form a crude tent where YERMA *sits.*

> [*The women enter, bringing offerings to the shrine. They are barefoot. In the group is the spirited* PAGAN OLD WOMAN *from Act One.*]

SONG:
> I couldn't see you
> When you were single,
> But now that you're married,
> I will find you.
> I'll strip you naked,
> Wife and pilgrim,
> When, in the dark,
> The clock strikes twelve.

PAGAN OLD WOMAN [*roguishly*]: Did you drink the holy water yet?

FIRST WOMAN: Yes.

PAGAN OLD WOMAN: And now, we'll see about this one.

SECOND WOMAN: We believe in him.

PAGAN OLD WOMAN: You all come to ask the Saint to give you children, and the result is that each year more men come alone on this pilgrimage. What goes on here? [*She laughs.*]

FIRST WOMAN: Why do you come here if you don't believe?

PAGAN OLD WOMAN: To watch. I love to watch! And to look after my son. Last year two men killed each other over one of these dried-up wives, and I want to keep an eye on him. And finally, I come because I feel like it!

FIRST WOMAN: May God forgive you!

[*The women exit.*]

PAGAN OLD WOMAN [*sarcastically, as she exits*]: May He forgive you!

[*She leaves.* MARIA *and the* FIRST GIRL *enter.*]

FIRST GIRL: Has she come?

MARIA: There is her cart. I had a hard time getting them to come. For the past month she hasn't been out of her chair. She frightens me! She has something in mind; I don't know what it is, but you can be sure it's nothing good!

FIRST GIRL: I came with my sister. She's been coming for eight years without results.

MARIA: You have children if you are meant to have them.

FIRST GIRL: That's what I say!

[*There are voices off-stage.*]

MARIA: I never liked this pilgrimage! Let's go to the threshing floor, that's where everyone is!

FIRST GIRL: Last year, when it got dark, some young men were grabbing my sister's breasts!

MARIA: For ten miles around, you hear nothing but filthy language!

FIRST GIRL: I saw more than forty barrels of wine in back of the shrine!

MARIA: A river of men without women flows down these mountains!

[*They exit. Off-stage voices.* YERMA *enters with six* WOMEN *who are going to the church. They are barefoot and carry spiral candles. Dusk begins to fall.*]

FIRST WOMAN:

Lord, let all the roses bloom,
Don't leave mine in the shade!

SECOND WOMAN:

Upon your withered flesh
The yellow rose will bloom.

THIRD WOMAN:

And in the womb of your servants,
The dark flame of the earth.

CHORUS OF WOMEN:

> Lord, let the roses bloom,
> Don't leave mine in the shade!

[*They kneel.*]

YERMA:

> Heaven is full of gardens
> With roses of happiness,
> And there among the roses
> Is one miraculous rose.
> It's like the light of morning;
> An archangel guards it well,
> With wings like enormous storm clouds,
> And eyes like agonies.
> And all around its petals,
> Springs of sweet, warm milk
> Frolic and bathe the faces
> Of the tranquil stars.
> Lord, open your rose
> Upon my withered flesh!

[*They get up.*]

SECOND WOMAN:

> Lord, cool with your hand
> The burning coals of her cheek!

YERMA:

> Listen to the penitent
> On your holy pilgrimage.
> Open your rose in my flesh,
> The rose with a thousand thorns.

CHORUS OF WOMEN:

> Lord, let the roses bloom,
> Don't leave mine in the shade!

YERMA:

> Over my withered flesh,
> One miraculous rose!

[*They exit. Four* YOUNG GIRLS *come running out from the*

left with long ribbons in their hands. From the right, three others with long ribbons, looking back over their shoulders. There is a crescendo of shouting and the sounds of cowbells and harness bells. On an upper level, the seven YOUNG GIRLS *wave their ribbons towards the left. The racket increases, as two mummers enter, one as a* MALE, *the other as a* FEMALE. *They wear large folk masks. The* MALE *clutches the horn of a bull in his hand. They are not grotesque in any way, but are of great beauty and pure earthiness. The* FEMALE *shakes a necklace of large jingle bells. Upstage, a crowd of people shouts and cheers the dancers on. Night has fallen.*]

CHILDREN:
> The devil and his wife! The devil and his wife!

FEMALE:
> In the river in the mountains,
> The despondent wife was bathing.
> Up along her naked body,
> Tiny water snails were climbing.
> The sand along the river edge,
> The breeze of early morning,
> Set her laughter all afire,
> Made her shoulders tremble.
> O she was naked, laughing,
> The maiden in the water!

BOY:
> O how she was moaning!

FIRST MAN:
> O thirsty for love!
> Dry, in the wind and the water!

SECOND MAN:
> Who is the one you're awaiting?

FIRST MAN:
> Who is the one you watch for?

SECOND MAN:

> O with your womb that is dry,
> And with your colour fading!

FEMALE:

> When night has come, I'll say it,
> When night has come, transparent,
> When night has come to the ritual,
> I'll tear my petticoats open!

BOY:

> And night was falling quickly.
> O how the night was falling!
> See how the darkness gathers
> At the waterfall on the mountain.

[*Guitars begin to play.*]

MALE [*rising and shaking the horn*]:

> O how white she is,
> The despondent wife!
> O how she moans in the branches!
> Later, she will be
> A poppy, a carnation –
> Later, when the male
> Opens up his cape.

[*He comes nearer.*]

> If you come to the ritual,
> Pray your womb will open.
> Don't put on a veil of mourning,
> Wear your softest, finest linen.
> Go alone behind the walls
> Where the fig-trees have been hidden.
> Lie beneath my earthen body
> Till the first white sigh of dawn.
> O how she is glowing!
> O how she was glowing!
> O how the wife is swaying!

FEMALE:
> O how love endows her
> With garlands and with crowns;
> And darts of molten gold
> Penetrate her breast!

MALE:
> Seven times she moaned
> And nine times she rose
> And fifteen times the jasmine
> Fused with the orange.

THIRD MAN:
> Strike her with the horn!

SECOND MAN:
> Again, the rose, the dance!

THIRD MAN:
> O how the wife is swaying!

MALE:
> In this ritual,
> The male takes command.
> Married men are bulls:
> The male takes command.
> Now, bestow the wreath –
> The pilgrim girls are flowers
> For the man who wins them!

BOY:
> Strike her with the wind!

SECOND MAN:
> Strike her with the wreath!

MALE:
> Come and see the glow
> Of the wife who was bathing!

THIRD MAN:
> She bends like a reed.

BOY:
> She fades like a flower.

MEN:
Let the little girls leave!

MALE:
Let them burn: the dance
And the glowing body
Of the innocent wife!

[*They are dancing off, smiling, to the sound of handclaps. They sing.*]

Heaven is full of gardens
With roses of happiness,
And there among the roses
Is one miraculous rose.

[*Two* YOUNG WOMEN *go by again, shouting. The cheerful* PAGAN OLD WOMAN *enters.*]

PAGAN OLD WOMAN: Let's see if you let us sleep later on! But later on, it will be her turn!

[YERMA *enters.*]

You!

[YERMA *is downcast, and does not speak.*]

Tell me, why did you come?

YERMA: I don't know.

PAGAN OLD WOMAN: You're not convinced? Where's your husband?

[YERMA *shows signs of exhaustion, and of being overcome by her obsession.*]

YERMA: He's over there.

PAGAN OLD WOMAN: What is he doing?

YERMA: Drinking. [*She pauses, then raises her hands to her forehead.*] Ai!

PAGAN OLD WOMAN: 'Ai!' 'Ai!' Less 'Ai!' and more spirit! I couldn't tell you anything before, but now I can.

YERMA: What are you going to tell me that I don't already know?

PAGAN OLD WOMAN: Something that can't be kept quiet any more. Something they are shouting from the rooftops! It's your husband's fault! Do you hear? They can cut off my hands! Neither his father, nor his grandfather, nor his great-grandfather, behaved like a breed of real men. Heaven and earth had to come together for them to have a son! They're put together with spit! Not like your people. You have brothers and cousins for a hundred miles around! See what a curse has fallen upon your beauty!

YERMA: A curse! A pool of poison over the wheat!

PAGAN OLD WOMAN: But you have feet – you can walk out of your house!

YERMA: Walk out?

PAGAN OLD WOMAN: When I saw you at the pilgrimage, my heart turned over! Women come here to find other men. And the Saint performs the miracle! My son is sitting behind the shrine waiting for you. My house needs a woman! Go with him and the three of us will live together. My son has good blood in his veins! Like me! If you come to my house, it still smells like cradles! The ashes of your bed-sheets will be bread and salt for your children. Go on! Don't worry about people. And as for your husband, there are enough brave hearts and sharp tools in my house to keep him from even crossing the street!

YERMA: Be quiet, be quiet, it's not that! I'd never do that! I can't go out looking. Do you think that I could have another man? What about my honour? You can't turn back the tide, or have a full moon come out at midday! Go away! I'll continue on the road I have chosen. Did you really think that I could turn to another man? That I'm going to beg like a slave for what belongs to me? Know who I am, so that you will never speak to me again! I am not looking for anyone.

PAGAN OLD WOMAN: When you're thirsty, you're grateful for water.

YERMA: I'm like a parched field big enough to hold a thousand teams of oxen ploughing, and what you give me is a little glass of water from the well! Mine is pain that is no longer of my flesh!

PAGAN OLD WOMAN [loudly]: Then go on this way. It's what you want! Like thistles in the wasteland – prickly, barren!

YERMA [*loudly*]: Barren, yes, I already know it! Barren! It's not necessary to rub my mouth in it! Don't amuse yourself like little children do with a dying animal! Ever since I got married, I've been turning that word over in my mind, but it's the first time I've heard it, the first time it's been said to my face! The first time I know that it's true!

PAGAN OLD WOMAN: I have no pity for you, none! I will look for another woman for my son!

[*She goes. A large chorus of pilgrims is singing in the distance.* YERMA *goes towards the cart, and her husband appears from behind it.*]

YERMA: You were there?

JUAN: I was.

YERMA: Listening?

JUAN: Listening.

YERMA: And you heard?

JUAN: Yes.

YERMA: What of it! Leave me alone and go join the singers! [*She sits down in the tent.*]

JUAN: It's also time for me to speak.

YERMA: Speak!

JUAN: And complain.

YERMA: About what?

JUAN: I have a bitterness in my throat.

YERMA: And I, in my bones!

JUAN: I can no longer put up with this constant grieving over obscure things, unreal things made of thin air.

YERMA [*dramatically*]: Unreal, you call it? Thin air, you call it?

JUAN: Over things that have not happened and that neither you nor I can control.

YERMA [*violently*]: Go on! Go on!

JUAN: Over things I don't care about! Do you hear? That I don't care about! I finally have to tell you! All I care about is what I can hold in my hands. What I can see with my eyes!

YERMA [*falling to her knees in desperation*]: That's it, that's it!

That's what I wanted to hear from your lips! You can't see the truth when it's inside you, but how huge it is, and how it screams, when it comes out and raises its arms! You don't care! At last I have heard it!

JUAN [*coming near her*]: Tell yourself it had to turn out this way. Listen to me!

[*He puts his arms around her to lift her to her feet.*]

Many women would be happy living the life you do. Life is sweeter without children! I'm happy not having them. We're not to blame in any way!

YERMA: Then what were you looking for in me?

JUAN: For you yourself!

YERMA [*with excitement*]: That's it! You were looking for a house, peace and quiet, and a wife! But nothing more. Is it true, what I'm saying?

JUAN: It's true! Like everyone.

YERMA: What about the rest? What about your son?

JUAN [*fiercely*]: Didn't you hear that I don't care? Don't ask me any more! I'll have to shout it in your ear for you to understand! Now let's see if once and for all you can live in peace!

YERMA: And you never considered having a son, when you saw how much I wanted one?

JUAN: Never!

[*They are both on the ground.*]

YERMA: And I have no hope?

JUAN: No.

YERMA: Nor you?

JUAN: Nor me either. Accept it!

YERMA: Barren!

JUAN: And we shall live in peace. Both of us, quietly, with pleasure. Embrace me!

[*He embraces her.*]

YERMA: What are you after?

JUAN: *You* are what I'm after! In the moonlight, you are beautiful!

YERMA: You pursue me as if I were a dove you want to devour!

JUAN: Kiss me – like this!

YERMA: Never! Never!

> [YERMA *cries out and clutches her husband by the throat. He falls back. She chokes him until she kills him. The pilgrims' chorus begins.*]

YERMA: Barren. Barren, but sure. Now I know it for certain. And alone.

> [*She stands up. People begin to gather.*]

I will sleep without suddenly waking up to see if my blood is proclaiming other, new blood. With my body dry forever. What do you want to know? Don't come near me, for I have killed my son! I myself have killed my son!

> [*A group gathers and stays upstage. We hear the pilgrims' chorus.*]

CURTAIN

THE HOUSE OF BERNARDA ALBA

A Drama of Women in the Villages of Spain

Cast of Characters

BERNARDA, age 60

MARIA JOSEFA (Bernarda's mother), age 80

ANGUSTIAS (Bernarda's daughter), age 39

MAGDALENA (Bernarda's daughter), age 30

AMELIA (Bernarda's daughter), age 27

MARTIRIO (Bernarda's daughter), age 24

ADELA (Bernarda's daughter), age 20

MAID, age 50

PONCIA (Maid), age 60

PRUDENCIA, age 50

BEGGAR WOMAN

LITTLE GIRL

WOMEN MOURNERS

FIRST WOMAN

SECOND WOMAN

THIRD WOMAN

FOURTH WOMAN

GIRL

The poet advises that these three acts are intended as a photographic documentary.

ACT ONE

A very white inner room in BERNARDA'*s house. Thick walls. Arched doorways with jute curtains trimmed with black beads and ruffles. Rush-bottomed chairs. Pictures of nymphs or legendary kings in improbable landscapes. It is summer. A great, shady silence envelops the stage. When the curtain rises, the stage is empty. Church bells are tolling.*

[*The* MAID *enters.*]

MAID: My head is bursting with those tolling bells!

PONCIA [*entering, eating bread and sausage*]: They've been mumbling away for more than two hours now. Priests have come from every town. The church looks beautiful! Magdalena fainted during the first response.

MAID: She's the one who's going to be the loneliest.

PONCIA: She's the only one her father loved. Oh, thank God we're alone for a moment! I came back here to eat.

MAID: If Bernarda should see you – !

PONCIA: Since she's not eating, she'd like it if we all starved. Bossy! Tyrant! But she'll be the loser – I've opened her jar of sausages.

MAID [*sadly, with longing*]: Poncia, why don't you give me some for my little girl?

PONCIA: Come take a handful of *garbanzos,** too. Today, she won't notice.

VOICE [*from within*]: Bernarda!

PONCIA: The old lady. Is she locked up tight?

MAID: With two turns of the key.

PONCIA: You should fasten the bolt, too. She has fingers like five skeleton keys!

* *Garbanzos*: chick-peas.

119

VOICE: Bernarda!

PONCIA [calling out]: She's coming! [To the MAID] Scrub everything clean. If Bernarda doesn't see things shine, she'll pull out the few hairs I have left!

MAID: What a woman!

PONCIA: She tyrannizes everyone around her. She could sit on your heart and watch you die for a whole year without taking that cold smile off her damn face! Scrub! Scrub those tiles!

MAID: My hands are bleeding from all this scouring.

PONCIA: She – the most immaculate – the most decent. She – the most superior! Her poor husband has earned a good rest.

[The bells stop tolling.]

MAID: Did all his relatives come?

PONCIA: Hers did. His people hate her. They came to see him dead and make the sign of the cross.

MAID: Are there enough chairs?

PONCIA: More than enough. Let them sit on the floor! Since Bernarda's father died, people haven't been back to this house. She doesn't want them to see her in her domain. Damn her!

MAID: She's been good to you.

PONCIA: Thirty years, washing her sheets. Thirty years, eating her leftovers. Nights watching over her when she coughs. Entire days peering through cracks, to spy on the neighbours and bring her the gossip. A life with no secrets from each other. And yet – damn her! May she have a horrible pain – like nails stuck in her eyes.

MAID: Poncia!

PONCIA: But I'm a good dog; I bark when I'm told to, and I snap at beggars' heels when she sets me on them. My sons work in her fields, and they're both married now, but some day I'll be sick of it.

MAID: And on that day . . .?

PONCIA: On that day I will lock myself in a room with her, and spit at her for a whole year! 'For this, Bernarda!' 'And for that!' 'And for the other!' Until she's like a lizard that children have smashed to pieces. That's what she is! And so is her whole family. I certainly don't envy the way she lives. She has five girls on her hands, five ugly daughters, but except for Angustias, the oldest – who is her first husband's child and has some money – the rest? Lots of fine lace, lots of linen shifts, but bread and grapes is all they will inherit!

MAID: I would like to have what they have.

PONCIA: What you and I have is our hands and a hole to be buried in when we die.

MAID: That's all the land they give to us who have nothing!

PONCIA [*at the cupboard*]: This crystal has some spots on it.

MAID: Neither soap nor flannel will get them off.

[*The bells ring.*]

PONCIA: The last prayer – I'm going over to listen. I love the way the priest sings! In the paternoster his voice rose higher and higher – like a water pitcher being filled little by little. Of course, at the end it cracked, but it's glorious to hear him. Even so, there's no one like Earsplitter, the old sacristan. He sang at the mass for my mother, may she rest in peace. The walls trembled, and when he sang the 'Amen', it was as if a wolf had come into the church. [*Imitating him*] AME-E-EN!! [*She starts to cough.*]

MAID: You'll pulverize your windpipe!

PONCIA: I'd rather pulverize something else!

[*She exits, laughing. The* MAID *scrubs. The bells ring.*]

MAID [*imitating the bells*]: Ding ding dong! Ding ding dong! May God forgive him.

BEGGAR WOMAN [*coming in with a* LITTLE GIRL]: Blessed be God!

MAID: Ding ding dong! Ding ding dong! May He wait many years for us! Ding ding dong!

BEGGAR WOMAN [*loudly, with a certain irritation*]: Blessed be God!

MAID [*irritated*]: Forever!

BEGGAR WOMAN: I've come for the leftovers.

[*The bells stop ringing.*]

MAID: You can get to the street right through that door. Today's leftovers are for me!

BEGGAR WOMAN: But you have someone to support you. My daughter and I are alone!

MAID: Dogs are alone, too, and they get by.

BEGGAR WOMAN: They always give them to me.

MAID: Get out of here! Who said you could come in? Now you've tracked up my floor.

[*They exit. The* MAID *continues scrubbing.*]

MAID: Floors polished with oil, cupboards, pedestals, steel beds. It's a bitter thing to swallow when you live in a mud hut with one plate and one spoon. I only hope some day not one of us will be left to tell about it.

[*The bells start ringing again.*]

Yes, yes, toll away! Bring in the coffin with its gold trim and the silk towels to carry it with. In the end you'll be the same as me. Rot away, Antonio María Benavides, stiff in your woven suit and your high boots! Rot away! Never again will you lift up my skirts behind the back corral!

[*From the rear,* WOMEN MOURNERS *begin to enter, two by two. They wear full black skirts and shawls and carry black fans. They enter slowly, until they fill the stage. The* MAID *breaks into a wail.*]

MAID: Oh, Antonio María Benavides, you'll never again see these walls, nor eat the bread of this house! Of those who served you, I loved you the most! [*She is tearing her hair.*] Must I go on living after you have gone? Must I go on living?

[*As the two hundred* WOMEN MOURNERS *finish entering,* BERNARDA ALBA *and her five* DAUGHTERS *appear.* BERNARDA *is leaning on a cane.*]

BERNARDA [*to the* MAID]: Silence!

MAID [*crying*]: Bernarda!

BERNARDA: Less screaming and more work! You should have seen to it everything was cleaner to receive the mourners. Get out! This is not where you belong.

[*The* MAID *leaves, weeping.*]

The poor are like animals; they seem to be made of other substances.

FIRST WOMAN: Poor people have their sorrows, too.

BERNARDA: But they forget them, once there's a plate of *garbanzos* in front of them!

GIRL [*timidly*]: You must eat to live.

BERNARDA: At your age, one does not speak in front of one's elders.

FIRST WOMAN: Be quiet, child!

BERNARDA: I have never let anyone lecture me. Sit down.

[*They sit. There is a pause.*]

BERNARDA: Magdalena, don't cry! If you want to cry, crawl under the bed. Did you hear me?

SECOND WOMAN [*to* BERNARDA]: Have you begun to thresh your wheat?

BERNARDA: Yesterday.

THIRD WOMAN: The sun beats down like lead.

FIRST WOMAN: I haven't known it to be this hot in years.

[*There is a pause. They all fan themselves.*]

BERNARDA: Is the lemonade ready?

PONCIA: Yes, Bernarda. [*She enters with a large tray full of small white cups, which she passes around.*]

BERNARDA: Give some to the men.

PONCIA: They're having some on the patio.

BERNARDA: Have them leave the way they came in. I don't want them coming through here.

GIRL [*to* ANGUSTIAS]: Pepe el Romano was with the men at the funeral.

ANGUSTIAS: He was there.

BERNARDA: His mother was there. She saw his mother. Neither she nor I saw Pepe.

GIRL: I thought I saw him.

BERNARDA: The one who *was* there was that widower from Darajalí. Standing very near to your aunt. All of us saw him.

SECOND WOMAN [*aside, in a low voice*]: Wicked! More than wicked!

THIRD WOMAN [*also in a low voice*]: A tongue like a knife!

BERNARDA: In church, women should look at no man but the priest, and at him only because he's wearing skirts. Whoever turns her head is on the prowl for a man.

FIRST WOMAN [*in a low voice*]: Dried-up old lizard!

PONCIA [*muttering*]: Twisted vine – reaching for the heat of a man!

BERNARDA [*striking the floor with her cane*]: Blessed be God!

ALL [*crossing themselves*]: Forever blessed and holy.

BERNARDA:
> Rest in peace, with the Heavenly
> Host watching over you.

ALL:
> Rest in peace!

BERNARDA:
> With Saint Michael the archangel
> And his sword of justice.

ALL:
> Rest in peace!

BERNARDA:
> With the key that opens all.
> And the hand that closes all.

ALL:
> Rest in peace!

BERNARDA:
> With all the blessed saints
> And the little lights of the fields.

ALL:
> Rest in peace!

BERNARDA:
> With our holy charity
> And the souls from land and sea.

ALL:
> Rest in peace!

BERNARDA: Grant repose to your servant Antonio María Benavides, and give him the crown of your sacred glory.

ALL:
> Amen!

BERNARDA [*getting to her feet and singing*]: *Requiem aeternam dona eis, Domine.*

ALL [*standing and singing in the Gregorian mode*]: *Et lux perpetua luceat eis.* [*They cross themselves.*]

FIRST WOMAN: Good health – to pray for his soul.
> [*They are filing out.*]

THIRD WOMAN: You'll never go without a hot loaf of bread.

SECOND WOMAN: Or shelter for your daughters.
> [*They all file past* BERNARDA *and leave.* ANGUSTIAS *exits through the patio door.*]

FOURTH WOMAN: May you continue to reap the harvest of your marriage.

PONCIA [*entering with a money bag*]: The men left this bag of money for prayers.

BERNARDA: Thank them, and pour them a glass of brandy.

GIRL [*to* MAGDALENA]: Magdalena . . .

BERNARDA [*to* MAGDALENA, *who is starting to cry*]: Sssh! [*She bangs her cane. To the guests, who have all left*] Go home and criticize everything you've seen! I hope many years go by before you cross my threshold again!

PONCIA: You have nothing to complain about. The whole town came!

BERNARDA: Yes – to fill my house with their sweaty underclothes and poisoned tongues!

AMELIA: Mother, don't talk like that!

BERNARDA: That's the way you must talk in this damned town without a river, this town of wells! Where you always drink the water fearing that it's poisoned!

PONCIA: Look what they've done to the floor!

BERNARDA: You would think a herd of goats had walked on it!

[PONCIA *scrubs the floor*.]

Adela, give me a fan.

ADELA: Here you are. [*She gives her a round fan decorated with red and green flowers.*]

BERNARDA [*hurling the fan to the floor*]: Is this the fan you give to a widow? Give me a black one, and learn to respect your father's memory!

MARTIRIO: Take mine.

BERNARDA: What about you?

MARTIRIO: I don't feel warm.

BERNARDA: Well, look for another – you're going to need one. During our eight years of mourning, no wind from the street will enter this house! Pretend we have sealed up the doors and windows with bricks. That was how it was in my father's house, and in my grandfather's house. In the meantime you can begin to embroider your trousseaus. I have twenty bolts of linen in the chest from which you can cut sheets. Magdalena can embroider them.

MAGDALENA: It's all the same to me.

ADELA [*acidly*]: If you don't want to embroider them, they'll go without embroidering. That way yours will stand out!

MAGDALENA: Neither mine nor yours. I know I'm not going to get married. I'd rather carry sacks to the mill. Anything but sit in this dark room, day after day!

BERNARDA: That's what it means to be a woman.

MAGDALENA: To hell with being a woman!

BERNARDA: Here you do what I tell you to do! You can't run to your father with your stories any more. A needle and thread for females: a mule and a whip for males. That's how it is for people born with means.

[ADELA *exits*.]

VOICE: Bernarda! Let me out!

BERNARDA [*in a loud voice*]: Let her out now!

[*The* MAID *enters*.]

MAID: I could hardly hold her. Your mother is eighty years old, but she's as strong as an oak.

BERNARDA: She takes after my grandfather. He was just the same.

MAID: Several times during the funeral I had to cover her mouth with an empty sack because she wanted to call out to you, to give her at least some dishwater to drink, and dog meat. That's what she says you give her.

MARTIRIO: She's up to no good.

BERNARDA [*to the* MAID]: She can let off steam out in the patio.

MAID: She took her rings and the amethyst earrings out of her trunk. She put them on and told me she wants to get married.

[*The* DAUGHTERS *laugh.*]

BERNARDA: Go with her, and be sure she doesn't go near the well.

MAID: Don't worry, she won't throw herself in!

BERNARDA: It's not that – out there, the neighbours can see her from their window.

[*The* MAID *exits.*]

MARTIRIO: We're going to change our clothes.

BERNARDA: Very well, but don't take the kerchief off your head.

[ADELA *enters.*]

Where is Angustias?

ADELA [*pointedly*]: I saw her peering through a crack in the front door. The men had just left.

BERNARDA: And you, why did you go to the door, too?

ADELA: I went to see if the hens had laid.

BERNARDA: But the men must have already left.

ADELA [*pointedly*]: A group of them were still standing around outside.

BERNARDA [*furious*]: Angustias! Angustias!

ANGUSTIAS [*as she enters*]: What do you want?

BERNARDA: What were you looking at? And who?

ANGUSTIAS: At no one.

BERNARDA: Is it proper for a woman of your class to go chasing after a man on the day of her father's funeral mass? Answer me! Who were you looking at?

[*There is a pause.*]

ANGUSTIAS: Me?

BERNARDA: You!

ANGUSTIAS: At no one.

BERNARDA [*advancing on her with her cane*]: You weakling!
  You're sickening! [*She strikes her.*]

PONCIA [*running to her*]: Bernarda, calm down!

  [*She holds on to her.* ANGUSTIAS *is crying.*]

BERNARDA: Get out of here! All of you!

  [*They all leave, except* BERNARDA *and* PONCIA.]

PONCIA: She did it without thinking what she was doing – which
  was clearly wrong. It seemed strange to me to see her sneaking
  off towards the patio. And then she stood at the window,
  listening to the men's conversation – which, as always, was not
  fit to hear.

BERNARDA: That's why they come to funerals. [*With curiosity*]
  What were they talking about?

PONCIA: They were talking about Paca la Roseta. Last night
  they tied her husband up in a stall, threw her over the back of
  a horse, and carried her off to the top of the olive grove.

BERNARDA: What about her?

PONCIA: Her? She agreed to it. They say she rode with her breasts
  hanging out, and Maximiliano held her as if he were playing a
  guitar. How horrible!

BERNARDA: Then what happened?

PONCIA: What was bound to happen. It was dawn when they got
  back. Paca la Roseta had her hair undone and was wearing a
  crown of flowers on her head.

BERNARDA: She's the only loose woman we have in this town.

PONCIA: Because she's not from here. She's from far away. And
  the men who went with her are the sons of strangers, too. The
  men around here wouldn't dare do that.

BERNARDA: No. But they like to watch it and talk about it, and
  lick their fingers over what goes on.

PONCIA: They said a lot more things.

BERNARDA [*glancing from side to side with a certain fear*]: What?

PONCIA: I'm embarrassed to mention them.

BERNARDA: And my daughter heard?

PONCIA: Of course!

BERNARDA: That one takes after her aunts. Soft and slippery – making sheep's eyes at any little barber who flattered them! How one must suffer and struggle to get people to behave decently and not like savages!

PONCIA: Your daughters are old enough to get married now. They give you little enough trouble. Angustias must be well over thirty by now.

BERNARDA: Thirty-nine, to be exact.

PONCIA: Imagine! And she's never had a suitor.

BERNARDA [*furious*]: None of them has had a suitor – or needs one! They can get by very well.

PONCIA: I didn't mean to offend you.

BERNARDA: For a hundred miles around, no one can measure up to them. The men here are not of their class. What would you have me do – turn them over to some field hand?

PONCIA: You should have gone to some other town.

BERNARDA: Of course – to sell them!

PONCIA: No, Bernarda, to change ... Of course, in other places, *they* would be the poor ones.

BERNARDA: Hold that vicious tongue!

PONCIA: No one can talk to you. Can we or can we not be honest with each other?

BERNARDA: We can not. You are my servant, and I pay you. Nothing more!

MAID [*entering*]: Don Arturo is here. He's come to discuss the will.

BERNARDA: Get busy! [*To the* MAID] You start scrubbing the patio. [*To* PONCIA] And you start putting away all the clothes of the deceased in the big chest.

PONCIA: We could give some things away.

BERNARDA: Nothing, not one button! Not even the handkerchief we used to cover his face!

[BERNARDA *leaves slowly, leaning on her cane, with a final look at the servants. Then the* MAIDS *exit.* AMELIA *and* MARTIRIO *enter.*]

AMELIA: Have you taken your medicine?

MARTIRIO: For all the good it's going to do me!

AMELIA: But you *have* taken it.

MARTIRIO: I do things I have no faith in, but I do them like clockwork.

AMELIA: You seem livelier since the new doctor arrived.

MARTIRIO: I feel the same.

AMELIA: Did you notice? Adelaida wasn't at the funeral.

MARTIRIO: I knew she wouldn't be. Her fiancé won't let her go out, not even to the front door. She used to be full of fun; now she doesn't even powder her face!

AMELIA: Nowadays, you don't know whether it's better to get engaged or not.

MARTIRIO: It's all the same.

AMELIA: The problem is we are always being criticized – they won't let us enjoy life. Adelaida must have had a terrible time.

MARTIRIO: She's afraid of Mother. She's the only one who knows the true story of her father and how he got his land. Every time she comes here, Mother needles her about it. Her father killed his first wife's husband in Cuba so he could marry her himself. Then, here, he deserted her and ran off with another woman, who had a daughter. And then he had an affair with this girl, Adelaida's mother, and he married her after his second wife went mad and died.

AMELIA: That despicable man, why isn't he in prison?

MARTIRIO: Because men cover up for each other, on this kind of thing, and no one dares to make accusations.

AMELIA: But Adelaida is not to blame for that.

MARTIRIO: No. But things have a way of repeating themselves. And I see how it all follows a terrible pattern. And she'll suffer the same fate as her mother and her grandmother – the two wives of the man who fathered her.

AMELIA: What an awful thing!

MARTIRIO: It's better never to lay eyes on a man. Since I was a child, I've been afraid of them. I used to see them in the corral, yoking the oxen and loading the sacks of wheat, with loud voices and clumsy feet, and I was always afraid of growing up for fear of suddenly finding myself in their clutches. God made me weak and ugly, and set them forever apart from me.

AMELIA: Don't say that! Enrique Humanas was after you and he used to like you.

MARTIRIO: The things people make up! One time I stood at the window in my nightgown until daylight because his field hand's daughter told me he was going to come, and he didn't. It was all just talk. Then he married someone with more money than me.

AMELIA: And ugly as the devil.

MARTIRIO: What do they care about ugliness? All they care about is land, oxen, and a meek little dog to cook for them.

[AMELIA *sighs*. MAGDALENA *enters*.]

MAGDALENA: What are you doing?

MARTIRIO: I'm just here.

AMELIA: And you?

MAGDALENA: I've been going through the rooms. To walk a little. To see the pictures grandmother embroidered on canvas – the little wool dog, the black man wrestling with the lion – that we liked so much when we were children. Those were happier times! A wedding lasted ten days and wagging tongues were not the fashion. Today there's more finesse, brides wear white veils like in the big cities, and we drink bottled wine. But inside we rot away over what people will say.

MARTIRIO: God knows what went on then!

AMELIA [*to* MAGDALENA]: One of your shoelaces is untied.

MAGDALENA: What difference does it make!

AMELIA: You'll step on it and you'll fall.

MAGDALENA: One less.

MARTIRIO: Where's Adela?

MAGDALENA: Ah! She put on the green dress she made to wear

on her birthday, she went out to the corral and began to shout, 'Chickens! Chickens, look at me!' I had to laugh.

AMELIA: If Mother had seen her!

MAGDALENA: Poor little thing! She's the youngest of us, and she has dreams. I would give anything to see her happy.

[*There is a pause.* ANGUSTIAS *crosses the stage carrying some towels.*]

ANGUSTIAS: What time is it?

MAGDALENA: It must be twelve by now.

ANGUSTIAS: So late?

AMELIA: It's just about to strike.

[ANGUSTIAS *exits.*]

MAGDALENA [*knowingly*]: Do you know about it yet? [*Indicating* ANGUSTIAS]

AMELIA: No.

MAGDALENA: Come on!

MARTIRIO: I don't know what you're referring to.

MAGDALENA: You two know more about it than I do. You always have your heads together like two little sheep, but you never confide in anyone else. About Pepe el Romano.

MARTIRIO: Ah!

MAGDALENA [*mimicking her*]: Ah! They are already talking about it in town. Pepe el Romano wants to marry Angustias. He was circling the house last night, and I think he'll send someone to ask for her hand soon.

MARTIRIO: I'm glad. He's good-looking.

AMELIA: Me, too. Angustias has good qualities.

MAGDALENA: Neither one of you is glad!

MARTIRIO: Magdalena! Really!

MAGDALENA: If he wanted Angustias for herself, Angustias as a woman, I would be glad. But he wants her money. Even though Angustias is our sister, in this family we know she's old, in poor health, and has always had the least to offer of any of us. After all, if she looked like a scarecrow when she was twenty, what can she look like now that she's forty?

MARTIRIO: Don't talk that way. Luck comes to the one who least expects it.

AMELIA: After all, she is telling the truth! Angustias has all her father's money. She is the only rich one in the house. That's why now that our father is dead and the estate is being settled, they're coming after her.

MAGDALENA: Pepe el Romano is twenty-five years old, and the best-looking man around. It would be natural for him to be interested in you, Amelia, or in our Adela, who is twenty years old, but not to come looking for the gloomiest person in this house – a woman who talks through her nose, like her father did!

MARTIRIO: Maybe he likes that!

MAGDALENA: I never could stand your hypocrisy!

MARTIRIO: God help us!

[ADELA enters.]

MAGDALENA: Have the chickens seen you yet?

ADELA: And what would you like me to do?

AMELIA: If Mother sees you, she'll drag you out by the hair.

ADELA: I had such dreams about this dress. I planned to wear it the day we were going out to eat water melons down by the water-wheel. There wouldn't have been another like it!

MARTIRIO: It's a lovely dress.

ADELA: And it suits me very well. It's the best one Magdalena has ever made.

MAGDALENA: What did the chickens say?

ADELA: They made me a gift of a few fleas that bit my legs.

[They laugh.]

MARTIRIO: What you could do is dye it black.

MAGDALENA: The best thing she could do is present it to Angustias to wear when she marries Pepe el Romano.

ADELA [with restrained emotion]: But Pepe el Romano . . .!

AMELIA: Haven't you heard?

ADELA: No.

MAGDALENA: Well, now you know!

ADELA: But that's not possible!

MAGDALENA: Money makes everything possible!

ADELA: Is that why she went out after the funeral and was looking through the door? [*She pauses.*] And that man has the nerve to . . .

MAGDALENA: He has the nerve to do anything.

[*There is a pause.*]

MARTIRIO: What are you thinking, Adela?

ADELA: I'm thinking that this period of mourning has caught me at the worst possible time.

MAGDALENA: You'll soon get used to it.

ADELA [*bursting into angry tears*]: I will not get used to it! I can't be locked up! I don't want my body to dry up like yours! I don't want to waste away and grow old in these rooms. Tomorrow I'll put on my green dress and go walking down the street. I want to get out!

[*The* MAID *enters.*]

MAGDALENA [*with authority*]: Adela!

MAID: The poor thing! How she misses her father . . .

[*She exits.*]

MARTIRIO: Be quiet!

AMELIA: What goes for one, goes for all!

[ADELA *calms down.*]

MAGDALENA: The maid almost heard you.

[*The* MAID *enters.*]

MAID: Pepe el Romano is coming down the street.

MAGDALENA: Let's go watch!

[AMELIA, MARTIRIO, MAGDALENA *run off quickly.*]

MAID [*to* ADELA]: You're not going?

ADELA: I don't care.

MAID: Since he'll be coming around the corner, you can see him better from the window in your room.

[*The* MAID *exits.* ADELA *hesitates for a moment, then she, too, rushes off towards her room.* BERNARDA *and* PONCIA *enter.*]

BERNARDA: That damned will!

PONCIA: What a lot of money was left to Angustias!

BERNARDA: Yes.

PONCIA: And to the others, so much less!

BERNARDA: You've said that to me three times now, and I didn't choose to answer you. So much less, a lot less – don't remind me of it again!

[ANGUSTIAS *enters. Her face is heavily powdered.*]

BERNARDA: Angustias!

ANGUSTIAS: Mother.

BERNARDA: Have you dared to powder your face? Have you dared even to *wash* your face, on the day of your father's death?

ANGUSTIAS: He was not my father! Mine died some time ago. Don't you remember him any more?

BERNARDA: You owe more to that man, the father of your sisters, than you do to your own. Thanks to that man, your future is assured.

ANGUSTIAS: We'll see about that!

BERNARDA: If only out of decency. Out of respect!

ANGUSTIAS: Mother, let me go!

BERNARDA: Go? After you've taken that powder off your face! Weakling! Hussy! You're the image of your aunts!

[*Furiously, she removes the powder from* ANGUSTIAS' *face with a handkerchief.*]

Now get out!

PONCIA: Bernarda, don't be so hard on her!

BERNARDA: My mother may have gone mad, but I am in control of myself. I know exactly what I'm doing.

[*The other* DAUGHTERS *enter.*]

MAGDALENA: What is going on?

BERNARDA: Nothing is going on.

MAGDALENA [*to* ANGUSTIAS]: If you're arguing about the inheritance – you're the richest, you keep it all.

ANGUSTIAS: Keep your tongue in its place!

BERNARDA [*rapping the floor with her cane*]: Don't entertain the illusion that you are going to be a match for me! Until I leave this house feet first, I will make the decisions – my own, and yours!

[*There are voices off-stage and* MARIA JOSEFA *enters, followed by the* MAID. *Bernarda's mother is a very old woman, decked out with flowers on her head and at her breast.*]

MARIA JOSEFA: Bernarda, where is my mantilla? I don't want any of you to have anything of mine. Not my rings nor my black moiré dress. Because none of you is going to get married. Not one! Bernarda, give me my pearl necklace!

BERNARDA [*to the* MAID]: Why did you let her in?

MAID [*trembling*]: She got away from me!

MARIA JOSEFA: I escaped because I want to get married, because I want to get married to a beautiful man from the edge of the sea. Since the men around here run away from women.

BERNARDA: Be quiet, Mother!

MARIA JOSEFA: No, I won't be quiet! I don't like to see these old maids, itching to get married, their hearts turning to dust. I want to go back to my own village! Bernarda, I want a man so I can get married and be happy!

BERNARDA: Lock her up!

MARIA JOSEFA: Let me come out, Bernarda!

[*The* MAID *takes hold of* MARIA JOSEFA.]

BERNARDA: Help her! All of you!

[*They all drag the old woman off the stage.*]

MARIA JOSEFA: I want to get away from here! Bernarda! To get married at the edge of the sea, at the edge of the sea!

FAST CURTAIN

End of Act One

ACT TWO

A white inner room in BERNARDA's *house. The doors at the left lead to the bedrooms.* BERNARDA's DAUGHTERS *except for* ADELA *are seated in low chairs, sewing.* MAGDALENA *is embroidering.* PONCIA *is with them.*

ANGUSTIAS: I've already cut the third sheet.

MARTIRIO: It's for Amelia.

MAGDALENA: Angustias, shall I put Pepe's initials on it, too?

ANGUSTIAS [*drily*]: No.

MAGDALENA [*calling out*]: Adela, aren't you coming?

AMELIA: She must be lying down.

PONCIA: Something's wrong with that girl. She seems restless, shaky, frightened – as if she had a lizard between her breasts!

MARTIRIO: There's nothing more nor less wrong with her than with any of us.

MAGDALENA: All of us except Angustias!

ANGUSTIAS: I feel just fine. And anyone who doesn't like it, can go to the devil!

MAGDALENA: Of course, one must admit the best things about you have always been your figure and your tact.

ANGUSTIAS: Fortunately, I'll soon be getting out of this hell!

MAGDALENA: Perhaps you won't be getting out.

MARTIRIO: Stop that talk!

ANGUSTIAS: And besides, gold in your purse is better than dark eyes in your face.

MAGDALENA: In one ear and out the other.

AMELIA [*to* PONCIA]: Open the door to the patio, to see if we can get a little fresh air.

[PONCIA *does so*.]

MARTIRIO: Last night it was so hot I couldn't get to sleep.

AMELIA: Neither could I.

MAGDALENA: I got up to cool off. There was a black storm cloud and even a few drops of rain.

PONCIA: It was one o'clock in the morning, and the heat was rising up out of the ground! I got up, too. Angustias was still at her window with Pepe.

MAGDALENA [*ironically*]: So late? What time did he leave?

ANGUSTIAS: Magdalena, why ask if you saw him?

AMELIA: He must have left about half past one.

ANGUSTIAS: Yes? How do *you* know?

AMELIA: I heard him cough, and I heard the pony stamping his hooves.

PONCIA: But I heard him leave around four o'clock.

ANGUSTIAS: That couldn't have been him.

PONCIA: I'm sure of it.

AMELIA: I thought so, too.

MAGDALENA: How very strange!

    [*There is a pause.*]

PONCIA: Tell me, Angustias – what did he say to you, the first time he came to your window?

ANGUSTIAS: Nothing. What would he say to me? It was just talk.

MARTIRIO: It really is strange how two people who have met suddenly see each other through a window grating and – just like that – they're engaged!

ANGUSTIAS: Well, it didn't bother me.

AMELIA: I'd feel – I don't know what.

ANGUSTIAS: Not me, because when a man approaches a window grating, he already knows – from people who come and go, who fetch and carry – that the answer will be yes.

MARTIRIO: Yes. But he must have asked!

ANGUSTIAS: Of course!

AMELIA [*with curiosity*]: And how did he ask you?

ANGUSTIAS: No special way – 'You already know why I'm here. I need a good woman, well-behaved, and that's you, if you agree.'

AMELIA: These things embarrass me!

ANGUSTIAS: And me, but you have to get through them.

PONCIA: Did he say any more?

ANGUSTIAS: Yes, he did all the talking.

MARTIRIO: What about you?

ANGUSTIAS: I couldn't. My heart almost jumped out of my mouth! It was the first time I was ever alone with a man at night.

MAGDALENA: And such a good-looking man!

ANGUSTIAS: He's not bad.

PONCIA: Such things are easy for people with a little experience, who talk and say things and wave their hands around. The first time my husband, Evaristo the Birdman, came to my window – ha, ha, ha!

AMELIA: What happened?

PONCIA: It was very dark. I saw him coming closer, and when he arrived, he said to me, 'Good evening.' 'Good evening,' I said to him, and we didn't speak for more than half an hour. The sweat was running down my whole body. Then Evaristo came closer and closer, as if he wanted to squeeze through the bars, and he said in a very low voice: 'Come here, so I can feel you!'

[*They all laugh.* AMELIA *jumps up and peers out of a door.*]

AMELIA: Oh! I thought Mother was coming.

MAGDALENA: She would have set us straight!

[*They go on laughing.*]

AMELIA: Sh-h-h-h . . .! She'll hear us!

PONCIA: Afterwards, he behaved himself. Instead of doing something else, he took up breeding finches – until he died. Anyway, it's best for single women like you to know that fifteen days after the wedding, a man leaves the bed for the table, then the table for the tavern. And any woman who doesn't accept it rots away crying in a corner!

AMELIA: You went along with it.

PONCIA: I could handle him!

MARTIRIO: Is it true, that you hit him, sometimes?

PONCIA: Yes, and I almost put his eye out!

MAGDALENA: That's how all women should be!

PONCIA: I'm from the same school as your mother. One day he said something or other to me, and I killed all his finches with the pestle from my kitchen mortar.

[*They laugh.*]

MAGDALENA: Adela, you shouldn't miss this!

AMELIA: Adela!

[*A pause*]

MAGDALENA: I'll go and see.

[*She exits.*]

PONCIA: That child is ill.

MARTIRIO: Of course. She hardly sleeps!

PONCIA: What does she do?

MARTIRIO: How do I know what she does!

PONCIA: You would know better than me, since you sleep with only a wall between you.

ANGUSTIAS: Envy is eating her up.

AMELIA: Don't exaggerate.

ANGUSTIAS: I see it in her eyes. She's beginning to look a little mad . . .

MARTIRIO: Don't talk about madness! This is the last place you can say that word!

[MAGDALENA *enters with* ADELA.]

MAGDALENA: Well – weren't you asleep?

ADELA: I don't feel well.

MARTIRIO [*insinuating*]: Didn't you sleep well last night?

ADELA: No.

MARTIRIO: Well, then?

ADELA [*loudly*]: Leave me alone! Asleep or awake, it's none of your business. I'll do what I want with my body.

MARTIRIO: It's only my concern for you!

ADELA: Concern? Or curiosity? Weren't you all sewing? Well, go on! I wish I were invisible, so I could walk through these rooms without being asked where I am going!

[*The* MAID *enters.*]

MAID: Bernarda is calling you. The man who sells lace is here.

[*They all exit, except* PONCIA *and* ADELA. *As* MARTIRIO *leaves, she stares fixedly at* ADELA.]

ADELA: Don't look at me any more! If you want, I'll give you my eyes – they are brighter – and my back, to fix that crooked one of yours. But turn your head away when I pass.

[MARTIRIO *exits*.]

PONCIA: Adela, she is your sister. Besides, she's the one who loves you the most.

ADELA: She follows me everywhere. Sometimes she peeks into my room to see if I'm asleep. She won't let me breathe! And it's always, 'What a shame about that face!' 'What a shame about that body, which will never belong to anyone!' No! My body will be for anyone I please.

PONCIA [*pointedly, confidentially*]: For Pepe el Romano. Isn't that it?

ADELA [*taken aback*]: What are you saying?

PONCIA: What I said, Adela.

ADELA: Be quiet!

PONCIA [*loudly*]: Do you think I haven't noticed?

ADELA: Lower your voice!

PONCIA: Get rid of those thoughts!

ADELA: What do you know?

PONCIA: Old women can see right through the walls. Where do you go at night when you get up?

ADELA: I wish you were blind!

PONCIA: I have eyes in my head and in my hands, when it comes to things like this. No matter how much I think about it, I can't figure out what you're up to. Why were you standing at the open window, half naked, with the light burning – the second time Pepe came to talk with your sister?

ADELA: That's not true!

PONCIA: Don't be childish. Leave your sister alone; and if you want Pepe el Romano, control yourself!

[ADELA *cries*.]

Besides, who says you can't marry him? Your sister Angustias is sickly. She won't survive even her first childbirth. She's narrow in the hips, old, and from what I know, I can tell she'll die. Then Pepe will do what all widowers do in this country: he'll marry the youngest, the most beautiful, and that will be you. Live on that hope or forget him, whatever you want – just don't go against the law of God!

ADELA: Be quiet!

PONCIA: I won't be quiet!

ADELA: Mind your own business! Spy! Traitor!

PONCIA: I'll have to be your shadow.

ADELA: Instead of cleaning the house and going to bed to pray for your dead, you go sticking your nose into the affairs of men and women like an old sow, so you can slobber over them.

PONCIA: I keep watch! So people won't spit when they come through that door.

ADELA: What great affection for my sister has suddenly come over you!

PONCIA: I have no affection for any of you, but I want to live in a decent house. I don't want to be disgraced in my old age.

ADELA: Your advice is useless – it's already too late! I wouldn't fight you – you're just a servant – I'd fight my mother, to put out this fire that rises from my legs and mouth. What can you say about me? That I lock myself in my room and don't open the door? That I don't sleep? I'm smarter than you are. See if you can catch this wild rabbit with your hands!

PONCIA: Don't defy me, Adela, don't defy me! Because I can raise my voice, light the lamps, and make the bells ring!

ADELA: Bring out four thousand yellow flares and set them on the walls of the corral. No one can keep what has to happen from happening!

PONCIA: You care about him that much!

ADELA: That much! When I look into his eyes, I feel as if I am slowly drinking in his blood!

PONCIA: I can't listen to you.

ADELA: Well, you *will* listen to me! I was afraid of you. But now

I'm stronger than you are.

[ANGUSTIAS *enters.*]

ANGUSTIAS: Always arguing!

PONCIA: Of course. She insists I go to the store in this heat to bring her I don't know what.

ANGUSTIAS: Did you buy me that bottle of perfume?

PONCIA: The most expensive. And the face-powder. I put them on the table in your room.

[ANGUSTIAS *exits.*]

ADELA: And hold your tongue!

PONCIA: We'll see about that!

[MARTIRIO, AMELIA *and* MAGDALENA *enter.*]

MAGDALENA [*to* ADELA]: Have you seen the lace?

AMELIA: The lace for Angustias' wedding sheets is beautiful.

ADELA [*to* MARTIRIO, *who is carrying some lace*]: And this?

MARTIRIO: It's for me. For a shift.

ADELA [*sarcastically*]: You have to have a sense of humour.

MARTIRIO [*pointedly*]: Just for me to see. I have no need to exhibit myself to anyone.

PONCIA: No one sees you in your shift.

MARTIRIO [*pointedly, looking at* ADELA]: Sometimes! But I adore underclothes! If I were rich, mine would be made of Dutch linen. It's one of the few pleasures I have left.

PONCIA: This lace is lovely for baby bonnets and christening gowns. I was never able to use it on mine. Now we'll see if Angustias uses it on hers. If she decides to have babies, you'll all be sewing morning and night!

MAGDALENA: I don't plan to sew a stitch!

AMELIA: Much less take care of someone else's children! Just look at the women down the street, sacrificing their lives for little brats!

PONCIA: They're better off than you. At least they laugh over there, and you can hear them bashing each other around.

MARTIRIO: Then go work for *them*!

PONCIA: No. I'm stuck in this convent now.

[*There is a jingling of bells in the distance.*]

MAGDALENA: It's the men coming back from the fields.

PONCIA: A minute ago it struck three!

MARTIRIO: With this sun!

ADELA [*sitting down*]: Oh, if only I could go out to the fields, too!

MAGDALENA [*sitting down*]: Each class does what it must.

MARTIRIO [*sitting down*]: That's how it is.

[AMELIA *sits down with a sigh.*]

PONCIA: There's no greater joy than being in the fields at this time of year! Yesterday morning the harvesters arrived. Forty or fifty good-looking young men.

MAGDALENA: Where are they from this year?

PONCIA: From very far away. They came from the hills. Full of spirit! Burnt like trees. Shouting and tossing stones! Last night a woman dressed in sequins arrived in town, and she danced to the accordion, and fifteen of them paid to take her into the olive grove. I saw them from a distance. The one who arranged it was a boy with green eyes, as tight as a sheaf of wheat.

AMELIA: Is it true?

ADELA: How can it be?

PONCIA: Years ago, another of these women came, and I myself gave money to my oldest son so he could go. Men need these things.

ADELA: They are forgiven everything!

AMELIA: To be born a woman is the worst punishment.

MAGDALENA: And not even our eyes belong to us.

[*There is singing in the distance, coming closer.*]

PONCIA: It's them. They have some lovely songs.

AMELIA: They're going out to harvest now.

[*Off-stage, tambourines and carrañacas play. There is a pause in the conversation; everyone listens in the sunstruck silence.*]

CHORUS [*off-stage*]:

> Harvesters going to reap the wheat,
> Going in search of the golden grain.

Reaping the hearts of the girls they meet,
Hearts they will harvest again.

AMELIA: And they don't mind this sun!

MARTIRIO: They harvest right through the blazing heat.

ADELA: I'd like to be a harvester, so I could come and go. Then I could forget what's eating away at us.

MARTIRIO: What do *you* have to forget?

ADELA: Each of us has something.

MARTIRIO [*intensely*]: Each of us!

PONCIA: Quiet! Quiet!

CHORUS [*at a distance*]:

Open your doors and your windows,
Ladies who live in this pueblo!
Harvesters beg for your roses,
Roses to trim their sombreros!

PONCIA: What singing!

MARTIRIO [*nostalgically*]:

Open your doors and your windows,
Ladies who live in this pueblo!

ADELA [*passionately*]:

Harvesters beg for your roses,
Roses to trim their sombreros!

[*The singing fades in the distance.*]

PONCIA: Now they're turning the corner.

ADELA: Let's go and watch them from the window in my room!

PONCIA: Be careful not to open it too wide – they're bold enough to give it a push to see who is looking.

[ADELA, MAGDALENA and PONCIA *leave.* MARTIRIO *stays seated in her chair with her head in her hands.*]

AMELIA [*going to her*]: What's the matter with you?

MARTIRIO: The heat makes me ill.

AMELIA: It's nothing more than that?

MARTIRIO: I wish November would come – the rainy days, the frost – anything but this interminable summer!

AMELIA: It will soon pass – and come again.

MARTIRIO: Of course. [*She pauses.*] What time did you fall asleep last night?

AMELIA: I don't know. I sleep like a log. Why?

MARTIRIO: No reason, except I thought I heard people in the corral.

AMELIA: Yes?

MARTIRIO: Very late.

AMELIA: And you weren't afraid?

MARTIRIO: No. I've heard it before, other nights.

AMELIA: We should be careful. Could it have been the field hands?

MARTIRIO: The field hands come at six.

AMELIA: Perhaps a little stray mule.

MARTIRIO [*muttering, with a double meaning*]: That's it, that's it! A little stray mule.

AMELIA: We have to warn the others.

MARTIRIO: No! No! Don't say anything! It could be I imagined it.

AMELIA: Perhaps.

    [*A pause.* AMELIA *starts to exit.*]

MARTIRIO: Amelia.

AMELIA [*at the door*]: What?

    [*There is a pause.*]

MARTIRIO: Nothing.

    [*A pause*]

AMELIA: Why did you call me?

    [*A pause*]

MARTIRIO: It slipped out. I didn't mean to.

    [*A pause*]

AMELIA: Lie down for a while.

ANGUSTIAS [*entering in a rage, in great contrast to the preceding silences*]: Where is the picture of Pepe I had under my pillow? Which of you has it?

MARTIRIO: Neither one of us.

AMELIA: It's not as if Pepe were a silver Saint Bartholomew.

    [PONCIA, MAGDALENA *and* ADELA *enter.*]

ANGUSTIAS: Where is the picture?

ADELA: What picture?

ANGUSTIAS: One of you has hidden it from me!

MAGDALENA: You have the effrontery to say that?

ANGUSTIAS: It was in my room, and now it's not!

MARTIRIO: Couldn't he have slipped out to the yard in the middle of the night? Pepe likes to walk around in the moonlight.

ANGUSTIAS: Don't play tricks on me! When he comes, I'm going to tell him!

PONCIA: Don't do that; it will turn up. [*Looking at* ADELA]

ANGUSTIAS: I would like to know which of you has it!

ADELA [*looking at* MARTIRIO]: Somebody! Anybody but me!

MARTIRIO [*pointedly*]: Of course!

BERNARDA [*entering*]: What is all this commotion in my house, and in the silence of this heavy heat? The neighbours must have their ears glued to the wall!

ANGUSTIAS: They have stolen my fiancé's picture!

BERNARDA [*fiercely*]: Who? Who?

ANGUSTIAS: Them!

BERNARDA: Which of you?

[*Silence*]

Answer me!

[*Silence. Then, to* PONCIA]

Search the rooms, look in the beds!

[PONCIA *exits.*]

This comes from not keeping you on a shorter leash! But I will haunt your dreams! [*To* ANGUSTIAS] Are you sure?

ANGUSTIAS: Yes.

BERNARDA: Have you looked for it carefully?

ANGUSTIAS: Yes, mother.

[*They are all standing in perplexed silence.*]

BERNARDA: At the end of my life, you make me drink the bitterest poison a mother can swallow! [*Calling out to* PONCIA] Can't you find it?

PONCIA [*entering*]: Here it is.

BERNARDA: Where did you find it?

PONCIA: It was . . .

BERNARDA: Don't be afraid to tell me.

PONCIA [*surprised*]: Between the sheets of Martirio's bed!

BERNARDA: Is that true?

MARTIRIO: It's true.

BERNARDA [*coming at her and hitting her with her cane*]: May God strike you dead, you two-faced scorpion! You thorn in my flesh!

MARTIRIO [*fiercely*]: Don't you hit me, Mother!

BERNARDA: As much as I want!

MARTIRIO: If I let you! Do you hear that? Get away!

PONCIA: Don't be disrespectful to your mother!

ANGUSTIAS [*seizing BERNARDA*]: Leave her alone! Please!

BERNARDA: There aren't even tears left in those eyes!

MARTIRIO: I'm not going to cry just to please you.

BERNARDA: Why did you take the picture?

MARTIRIO: Can't I play a joke on my own sister? Why would I want it?

ADELA [*exploding with jealousy*]: It was not a joke – you've never liked games, never! It was something else, exploding in your heart, wanting to come out! Admit it openly, once and for all!

MARTIRIO: Be quiet, don't make me talk! Because if I talk, the walls will collapse in shame!

ADELA: A vicious tongue never stops lying!

BERNARDA: Adela!

MAGDALENA: You are both crazy!

AMELIA: And you torture us with your sinful thoughts!

MARTIRIO: Others do things that are even more sinful!

ADELA: Until they strip themselves naked, and let the river sweep them away!

BERNARDA: Shameless!

ANGUSTIAS: It's not my fault that Pepe el Romano has chosen me!

ADELA: For your money!

ANGUSTIAS: Mother!

BERNARDA: Silence!

MARTIRIO: For your fields and your orchards.

MAGDALENA: That's the truth!

BERNARDA: Silence, I said! I saw the storm coming, but I didn't think it would burst so soon. Oh, what a hailstone of hate you have dropped on my heart! But I'm not old yet, and I have five chains for you, and this house my father built, so not even the weeds will know of my desolation. Get out of here!

[*They leave.* BERNARDA *sits down, desolate.* PONCIA *is standing close to the wall.* BERNARDA *collects herself and strikes the floor with her cane.*]

I must use a firm hand with them. Bernarda, remember: this is your duty!

PONCIA: May I speak?

BERNARDA: Speak. I'm sorry you heard. It's never wise to let an outsider into the family circle.

PONCIA: What I have seen, I have seen.

BERNARDA: Angustias must get married right away.

PONCIA: Of course. We have to get her away from here.

BERNARDA: Not her. Him!

PONCIA: Of course. We must get him far away from here. Good thinking!

BERNARDA: I don't think. There are things we cannot and should not *think*! I give orders.

PONCIA: And do you believe he'll want to leave?

BERNARDA [*getting up*]: What's going on in that head of yours?

PONCIA: He – of course! – will marry Angustias.

BERNARDA: Go on! I know you well enough to see you already have your knife out.

PONCIA: I never thought giving a warning would be called murder.

BERNARDA: You have something to warn me about?

PONCIA: I'm not making accusations, Bernarda. I'm only telling you: open your eyes and you'll see.

BERNARDA: See what?

PONCIA: You've always been clever. You can see evil in people from a hundred miles away. I have often believed you could read people's minds. But your children are your children. And about them, you are blind.

BERNARDA: Are you referring to Martirio?

PONCIA: Well, when it comes to Martirio ... [*with curiosity*] Why would she hide the picture?

BERNARDA [*wanting to cover up for her daughter*]: After all, she says it was a joke. What else could it be?

PONCIA [*sarcastically*]: Do you believe that?

BERNARDA [*vigorously*]: I don't *believe* it – it is so!

PONCIA: All right – it's your family we're dealing with. But if it were the neighbour across the street – what would you think?

BERNARDA: Now you're beginning to sharpen your knife.

PONCIA [*with unrelenting cruelty*]: Bernarda, something monstrous is happening here. I don't want to blame you, but you haven't allowed your daughters any freedom. Martirio is romantic, no matter what you say. Why didn't you let her marry Enrique Humanas? Why did you send him a message not to come to her window, the very day he was coming?

BERNARDA [*loudly*]: And I would do it a thousand times again! My blood will never mix with that of the Humanas family – not as long as I live! His father was a field hand.

PONCIA: This is what comes of putting on airs!

BERNARDA: I do because I can afford to! And you don't because you know very well what you come from.

PONCIA [*with hatred*]: Don't remind me of that! I'm old now. I've always been grateful for your protection.

BERNARDA [*drawing herself up*]: It wouldn't seem so!

PONCIA [*with hatred masked in sweetness*]: Martirio will forget about this.

BERNARDA: And if she doesn't forget, the worse for her! I don't think this is the 'something monstrous' happening here. Nothing is happening here. That's what you'd like. And if something does happen some day, rest assured it will not go beyond these walls!

PONCIA: I don't know about that – there are also people in town who can read hidden thoughts from a distance.

BERNARDA: How you'd like to see my daughters and me on our way to the whore-house!

PONCIA: No one can know her own fate.

BERNARDA: I know my fate – and that of my daughters. We'll leave the brothel to a certain woman who is already dead.

PONCIA [*fiercely*]: Bernarda, respect the memory of my mother!

BERNARDA: Stop hounding me, you with your evil thoughts!

[*There is a pause.*]

PONCIA: It's best if I don't get mixed up in anything.

BERNARDA: That's what you should do: work and keep your mouth shut. It is the obligation of those who are paid to work.

PONCIA: But I can't. Don't you think that Pepe would be better off married to Martirio or – Yes! to Adela?

BERNARDA: I do *not* think so.

PONCIA [*pointedly*]: Adela. She's el Romano's real fiancée.

BERNARDA: Things are never the way we would like them to be.

PONCIA: But it's very hard for people to turn away from their true inclinations. For Pepe to be with Angustias seems wrong – to me, and to other people, and even to the air. Who knows if they'll get their way!

BERNARDA: Here we go again! You go out of your way to give me bad dreams. And I don't want to listen to you, because if things turn out the way you say, I will have to claw you to pieces!

PONCIA: The blood wouldn't get as far as the river!

BERNARDA: Fortunately, my daughters respect me and have never gone against my will.

PONCIA: That's true. But as soon as you turn them loose, they'll be up on the roof.

BERNARDA: I will bring them down soon enough, by throwing stones at them!

THE HOUSE OF BERNARDA ALBA

PONCIA: Of course you are the strongest!

BERNARDA: I've always been able to hold my own.

PONCIA: But it's strange! At her age! Look at how taken Angustias is with her fiancé! And he seems to be smitten, too! Yesterday, my oldest son told me that at half past four in the morning, when he went by with his oxen, they were still talking!

BERNARDA: At half past four?

ANGUSTIAS [entering]: That's a lie!

PONCIA: That's what I was told.

BERNARDA [to ANGUSTIAS]: Go on!

ANGUSTIAS: For more than a week, Pepe has been leaving here at one o'clock. May God strike me dead if I'm lying!

MARTIRIO [entering]: I heard him leave at four, too.

BERNARDA: But did you see him with your own eyes?

MARTIRIO: I didn't want to be seen. Don't you usually talk through the window facing the alley?

ANGUSTIAS: I talk through the window in my bedroom.

[ADELA appears at the door.]

MARTIRIO: Then . . .

BERNARDA: What is going on here?

PONCIA: Careful, you'll find out! But it's clear Pepe was at one of the windows of your house at four in the morning.

BERNARDA: Do you know that for certain?

PONCIA: You don't know anything for certain in this life.

ADELA: Mother, don't listen to someone who wants to destroy us all!

BERNARDA: I will know how to find out. If people in this town want to bear false witness, they will find me as hard as flint. This matter is not to be discussed. Sometimes other people stir up a wave of mud in order to destroy us.

MARTIRIO: I don't like to lie.

PONCIA: Then something *is* going on.

BERNARDA: Nothing is going on. I was born with my eyes open. Now I'll keep watch, and never close them until I die.

ANGUSTIAS: I have the right to know!

BERNARDA: You have no right except to obey! No one is going to push me or pull me. [*To* PONCIA] And you take care of your own affairs. Here, no one will take one step without my knowing it!

MAID [*entering*]: There's a big crowd up the street! And all the neighbours are at their doors!

BERNARDA [*to* PONCIA]: Run and find out what's happening!

[*The women start to hurry off.*]

Where are you going? I always knew you were busybodies who would break your mourning. All of you, to the patio!

[*They exit first, and then* BERNARDA. *We hear distant voices.* MARTIRIO *and* ADELA *enter. They stand listening, not daring to take another step towards the outside door.*]

MARTIRIO: Be grateful I didn't happen to open my mouth.

ADELA: I could have said things, too.

MARTIRIO: And what could you say? Wanting is not doing.

ADELA: She who can, does – and she who takes the first step ... You wanted to, but you couldn't.

MARTIRIO: You won't go on like this much longer.

ADELA: I'll have it all!

MARTIRIO: I'll tear you out of his arms!

ADELA [*pleading*]: Martirio, leave me alone!

MARTIRIO: Never!

ADELA: He wants me in his house!

MARTIRIO: I saw the way he embraced you!

ADELA: I didn't want to! It was like being dragged by a rope.

MARTIRIO: You'd be better off dead!

[MAGDALENA *and* ANGUSTIAS *appear. The crowd noises grow louder.*]

PONCIA [*entering with* BERNARDA]: Bernarda!

BERNARDA: What is going on?

PONCIA: Librada's daughter, the one who's not married, just had a baby, and no one knows who the father is!

ADELA: A baby?

PONCIA: And to hide her shame, she killed it and put it under some rocks. But some dogs, with more feelings than many creatures, pulled it out, and as if led by the hand of God, they put it on her doorstep. Now they want to kill her. They're dragging her down the street, and the men are running down the paths and out of the olive groves, shouting so loud the fields are trembling.

BERNARDA: Yes! Let them all bring whips made from olive branches and the handles of their hoes! Let them all come to kill her!

ADELA: No. No! Not to kill her!

MARTIRIO: Yes, let's go out there, too!

BERNARDA: Any woman who tramples on decency should pay for it!

[Outside, a woman screams, and there is a great uproar.]

ADELA: They should let her go! Don't go out there!

MARTIRIO [looking at ADELA]: She should pay for what she did.

BERNARDA [in the archway]: Finish her off before the police get here! Burning coals in the place where she sinned!

ADELA [clutching her womb]: No! No!

BERNARDA: Kill her! Kill her!

CURTAIN

End of Act Two

ACT THREE

The interior patio of BERNARD's house. It is night. Four white walls lightly bathed in blue. The décor must be one of perfect simplicity. The doors, illuminated by the light from inside, cast a delicate glow on the scene. At centre, a table with an oil-lamp where BERNARDA *and her* DAUGHTERS *are eating.* PONCIA *is serving them.* PRUDENCIA *is seated at one side. The curtain rises on total silence, interrupted only by the clatter of dishes and cutlery.*

PRUDENCIA: I'm going now. It's been a long visit. [*She rises.*]

BERNARDA: Wait, Prudencia! We never see each other.

PRUDENCIA: Has the last call for the rosary sounded?

PONCIA: Not yet.

[PRUDENCIA *sits down.*]

BERNARDA: How is your husband getting on?

PRUDENCIA: The same.

BERNARDA: We don't see him, either.

PRUDENCIA: You know how he is. Ever since he fought with his brothers over the inheritance, he hasn't used the front door. He puts up a ladder and climbs over the wall and the corral.

BERNARDA: He's a real man! And with your daughter?

PRUDENCIA: He has not forgiven her.

BERNARDA: He is right.

PRUDENCIA: I don't know what to tell you. I suffer because of it.

BERNARDA: A daughter who disobeys stops being a daughter and becomes an enemy.

PRUDENCIA: I just let the water flow. The only comfort I have left is to take refuge in the church, but since my eyes are failing, I'll have to stop coming, because the children tease me.

[*There is a loud thud from the other side of the wall.*]

PRUDENCIA: What is that?

BERNARDA: The breeding stallion, locked up and kicking the wall. [*Loudly*] Shackle him and let him out in the corral! [*Confidentially*] He must be hot.

PRUDENCIA: Are you going to breed him with your new mares?

BERNARDA: At sunrise.

PRUDENCIA: You've been good at building up your herd.

BERNARDA: Thanks to money and a lot of unpleasantness.

PONCIA [*interrupting*]: But she has the best herd in this part of the country. It's too bad prices are down.

BERNARDA: Would you like some cheese and honey?

PRUDENCIA: I have no appetite.

[*There is another thud.*]

PONCIA: For God's sake!

PRUDENCIA: It made my heart pound!

BERNARDA [*rising furiously*]: Must I say things twice? Let him out so he can roll around in the piles of straw. [*After a pause, as if speaking to the hired hands*] Well, shut the mares in the stable, but turn him loose before he kicks down the walls! [*She goes back to the table and sits.*] Oh, what a life!

PRUDENCIA: Struggling like a man.

BERNARDA: That's the way it is.

[ADELA *gets up from the table.*]

Where are you going?

ADELA: For a drink of water.

BERNARDA [*calling out*]: Bring a pitcher of cool water! [*To* ADELA] You may sit down.

[ADELA *sits down.*]

PRUDENCIA: What about Angustias, when will she get married?

BERNARDA: They are coming to ask for her hand in three days.

PRUDENCIA: You must be pleased!

ANGUSTIAS: Of course!

ADELA [*to* MAGDALENA]: Now you've spilled the salt!

MAGDALENA: Your luck can't get any worse than it is now.

AMELIA: It's always a bad sign.

BERNARDA: That's enough!

PRUDENCIA [*to* ANGUSTIAS]: Has he given you the ring yet?

ANGUSTIAS: Do look at it. [*She holds it out.*]

PRUDENCIA: It's lovely. Three pearls! In my day, pearls meant tears.

ANGUSTIAS: But things have changed now.

ADELA: I don't think so. Things always mean the same. Engagement rings are supposed to be diamonds.

PRUDENCIA: It's more appropriate.

BERNARDA: With pearls or without them, things are what you make of them.

MARTIRIO: Or what God makes of them.

PRUDENCIA: Your furniture, they tell me, is lovely.

BERNARDA: I spent sixteen thousand *reales*.

PONCIA [*interjecting*]: The best is the mirrored wardrobe.

PRUDENCIA: I never saw one of those fancy things.

BERNARDA: All we had was a chest.

PRUDENCIA: What's important is that things work out.

ADELA: And you never know.

BERNARDA: There's no reason why it shouldn't.

[*Bells are heard, very far off.*]

PRUDENCIA: The last call. [*To* ANGUSTIAS] I'll come back soon, so you can show me the clothes.

ANGUSTIAS: Whenever you like.

PRUDENCIA: Good night. God be with you.

BERNARDA: Goodbye, Prudencia.

DAUGHTERS [*together*]: God go with you.

[*There is a pause.* PRUDENCIA *leaves.*]

BERNARDA: We are through eating now.

[*They get up from the table.*]

ADELA: I'm going to the front door to stretch my legs and get a little fresh air.

[MAGDALENA *sits in a low chair against the wall.*]

AMELIA: I'll go with you.

MARTIRIO: Me, too.

ADELA [*with repressed hatred*]: I'm not going to get lost.

AMELIA: You should have company at night.

[*They go out.* BERNARDA *sits.* ANGUSTIAS *is clearing the table.*]

BERNARDA: I've already told you I want you to speak to your sister Martirio. What happened with the picture was just a joke, and you should forget it.

ANGUSTIAS: You know she doesn't love me.

BERNARDA: We each know what we're thinking inside. I don't pry into people's feelings, but I do want to keep up appearances and have harmony in the family. Do you understand that?

ANGUSTIAS: Yes.

BERNARDA: That's settled, then.

MAGDALENA [*half asleep*]: Anyway, you're going to be leaving very soon! [*She falls asleep.*]

ANGUSTIAS: Not soon enough, I feel!

BERNARDA: What time did you finish talking last night?

ANGUSTIAS: At half past twelve.

BERNARDA: What does Pepe have to say?

ANGUSTIAS: I find him distracted. He always talks to me as if he's thinking of something else. If I ask him what's wrong, he answers, 'We men have our own worries.'

BERNARDA: You shouldn't ask him. Especially after you're married. Speak if he speaks, and look at him when he looks at you. That way you won't quarrel.

ANGUSTIAS: Mother, I think he hides many things from me.

BERNARDA: Don't try to find out about them. Don't ask him. And above all, don't ever let him see you cry.

ANGUSTIAS: I should be happy, and I'm not.

BERNARDA: It's all the same.

ANGUSTIAS: I often stare very hard at Pepe, until he grows blurred behind the bars of the window, as if he were being covered by a cloud of dust like the ones the sheep stir up.

BERNARDA: It's only because you're frail.

ANGUSTIAS: I hope so.

BERNARDA: Is he coming tonight?

ANGUSTIAS: No. He went to the city with his mother.

BERNARDA: Then we'll get to bed earlier. Magdalena!

ANGUSTIAS: She's asleep.

[ADELA, MARTIRIO *and* AMELIA *enter.*]

AMELIA: What a dark night!

ADELA: You can't see two steps ahead of you.

MARTIRIO: A good night for thieves, for someone who needs a hiding-place.

ADELA: The stallion was in the middle of the corral – so white! Twice as big, completely filling the darkness!

AMELIA: It's true. It was frightening! It was like an apparition.

ADELA: There are stars in the sky as big as fists!

MARTIRIO: Our sister was staring so hard at them, she almost broke her neck.

ADELA: Don't you like them?

MARTIRIO: I don't care what goes on above the rooftops. I have enough with what goes on inside these rooms!

ADELA: That's how you are.

BERNARDA: She has her way and you have yours.

ANGUSTIAS: Good night.

ADELA: Are you going to bed now?

ANGUSTIAS: Yes. Pepe is not coming tonight.

[*She exits.*]

ADELA: Mother, when there's a shooting star or a flash of lightning, why do we say:

> 'Blessed Saint Barbara, why
> Are you writing, up so high,
> With holy water in the sky?'

BERNARDA: In the old days they knew many things that we have forgotten.

AMELIA: I close my eyes so I won't see them!

ADELA: Not me. I like to see things blazing through the sky, after being motionless year after year.

MARTIRIO: But these things have nothing to do with us.

BERNARDA: And it's best not to think about them.

ADELA: What a beautiful night! I'd like to stay up very late so I could enjoy the cool air from the fields.

BERNARDA: But we have to go to bed. Magdalena!

AMELIA: She dozed off.

BERNARDA: Magdalena!

MAGDALENA [*annoyed*]: Leave me in peace.

BERNARDA: Go to bed!

MAGDALENA [*getting up peevishly*]: You don't leave a person alone!

[*She leaves, grumbling.*]

AMELIA: Good night.

[*She goes.*]

BERNARDA: You go, too.

MARTIRIO: Why isn't Angustias' fiancé coming tonight?

BERNARDA: He went on a trip.

MARTIRIO [*looking at* ADELA]: Ah!

ADELA: See you in the morning.

[*She leaves.* MARTIRIO *drinks some water and exits slowly, looking towards the door to the corral.*]

PONCIA [*entering*]: Are you still here?

BERNARDA: Enjoying this silence, and unable to find any trace of that 'monstrous thing' you claim is happening here.

PONCIA: Bernarda, let's forget about that conversation.

BERNARDA: In this house there is no question of 'yes' or 'no'. My vigilance takes care of that.

PONCIA: Nothing is happening on the surface, it's true. Your daughters are tucked away in a cupboard, and that's how they live. But neither you nor anyone else can see into their hearts.

BERNARDA: My daughters breathe easily.

PONCIA: You care about that because you're their mother. For me, looking after your house is enough.

BERNARDA: Now you've decided to become silent!

PONCIA: I know my place, and I'm at peace.

BERNARDA: The trouble is, you have nothing to talk about. If there were grass growing in this house, you'd bring every sheep in the neighbourhood in to graze.

PONCIA: I cover up more than you think.

BERNARDA: Does your son still see Pepe at four o'clock in the morning? Do they still tell the same malicious stories about this house?

PONCIA: They say nothing.

BERNARDA: Because they can't! Because there's no meat to bite into. Thanks to my watchful eyes.

PONCIA: Bernarda — I don't want to talk, because I'm afraid of what you'll do. But don't be too sure.

BERNARDA: Absolutely sure!

PONCIA: When you least expect it, lightning strikes! When you least expect it, your heart stops!

BERNARDA: Nothing is happening here! I'm quite prepared to deal with your suppositions.

PONCIA: Well, all the better for you!

BERNARDA: All the better!

MAID [*entering*]: I have finished washing the dishes now. Is there anything else you want, Bernarda?

BERNARDA [*getting up*]: Nothing. I'm going to bed.

MAID: What time do you want me to call you?

BERNARDA: Don't. Tonight I'm going to sleep well.
    [*She exits.*]

PONCIA: When you can't fight the tide, it's easier to turn your back, so you don't see it.

MAID: She's so proud she puts a blindfold on herself.

PONCIA: There's nothing I can do. I tried to put a stop to all this, but now it frightens me too much. Do you hear this silence? Well, there's a storm brewing in every room. The day it bursts, we'll all be swept away! I've said what I had to say.

MAID: Bernarda thinks that no one can stand up to her. She doesn't realize the power a man can have over lonely women.

PONCIA: It's not all Pepe el Romano's fault. It's true that last year he was after Adela, and she was crazy for him. But she should have known her place and not led him on. A man is a man.

MAID: They say he spoke to Adela many times.

PONCIA: It's true. [*Lowering her voice*] And other things.

MAID: I don't know what's going to happen here.

PONCIA: I'd like to cross the ocean and get away from this house of turmoil.

MAID: Bernarda is rushing the wedding day, and perhaps nothing will happen.

PONCIA: Things have already gone too far. Adela has made up her mind to do whatever it takes, and the others keep watch, all the time.

MAID: Martirio, too?

PONCIA: She's the worst! She's a well of poison! She knows el Romano is not for her, and she would crush the world if it were in her hand.

MAID: They are wicked.

PONCIA: They are women without men, that's all. When it comes to that, you even forget your own blood. Ssssssh! [*She listens.*]

MAID: What is it?

PONCIA [*stands up*]: The dogs are barking.

MAID: Someone must have walked past the front door.

[ADELA *enters, wearing white petticoats and a bodice.*]

PONCIA: Didn't you go to bed?

ADELA: I'm getting a drink of water. [*She drinks from a glass on the table.*]

PONCIA: I thought you were asleep.

ADELA: I woke up thirsty. And what about you, aren't you going to get some rest?

MAID: Right away.

[ADELA *exits.*]

PONCIA: Let's go.

MAID: We've earned our sleep. Bernarda doesn't give me a moment's rest the whole day.

PONCIA: Take the lamp with you.

MAID: The dogs are barking like mad!

PONCIA: They're not going to let us sleep.

[*They exit. The stage is almost dark.* MARIA JOSEFA *enters, carrying a baby ewe* in her arms.*]

---

*Ovejita ('Oh-vey-HEE-tah'): baby ewe.

MARIA JOSEFA:

>*Ovejita*, child of mine,
>Come with me to the edge of the sea.
>The little ant is at his door,
>I'll give you my breast, and bread.

>Bernarda –
>Face of a leopard.
>Magdalena –
>Face of a hyena.
>*Ovejita* –
>Baa-baa-baa, baa-baa-baa.
>We'll go to the palms at the gates of Bethlehem.

>You and I don't want to sleep;
>The door will open on its own
>And you and I will hide ourselves
>In a hut made of coral on the beach.

>Bernarda –
>Face of a leopard.
>Magdalena –
>Face of a hyena.
>*Ovejita* –
>Baa-baa-baa, baa-baa-baa.
>We'll go to the palms at the gates of Bethlehem.

[*She leaves, singing.* ADELA *enters. She looks furtively from side to side and disappears through the door to the corral.* MARTIRIO *enters through another door and stands, waiting in anguish, at the centre of the stage. She, too, is in petticoats. She's wearing a black shawl with the ends tucked tightly at her waist.* MARIA JOSEFA *enters down stage of her.*]

MARTIRIO: Grandmother, where are you going?

MARIA JOSEFA: Are you going to open the door for me? Who are you?

MARTIRIO: How did you get here?

MARIA JOSEFA: I escaped. Who are you?

MARTIRIO: Go to bed.

MARIA JOSEFA: You're Martirio, now I see you. Martirio, face of a martyr. And when are you going to have a child? I've had this one.

MARTIRIO: Where did you get that lamb?

MARIA JOSEFA: I know it's a lamb. But why can't a lamb be a child? It's better to have a lamb than to have nothing. Bernarda, face of a leopard; Magdalena, face of a hyena.

MARTIRIO: Don't talk so loud.

MARIA JOSEFA: It's true. Everything is very dark. Just because I have white hair you think I can't have babies. And – yes! Babies and babies and babies! This child will have white hair, and have another child, and that one, another, and all of us with hair of snow will be like the waves, one after another after another. Then we'll all settle down, and we'll all have white hair, and we'll be foam on the sea. Why isn't there any white foam here? Here, there's nothing but black mourning shawls.

MARTIRIO: Be quiet, be quiet!

MARIA JOSEFA: When my neighbour had a child, I used to take chocolate to her, and then she would bring some to me, and so on – forever and ever and ever! You will have white hair, but the neighbours won't come. I have to go, but I'm afraid the dogs will bite me. Will you come with me out to the fields? I don't like the fields. I love houses, but houses that are open, and the men are outside, sitting on their chairs. Pepe el Romano is a giant! You all want him. But he is going to devour you, because you're grains of wheat. Not grains of wheat! Frogs without tongues!

MARTIRIO [*emphatically*]: Come on. Go to bed. [*She pushes her.*]

MARIA JOSEFA: Yes, but later you'll let me out, won't you?

MARTIRIO: Of course.

MARIA JOSEFA [*weeping*]:
> *Ovejita*, child of mine,

Come with me to the edge of the sea.
The little ant is at his door,
I'll give you my breast, and bread.

[MARTIRIO *locks the door through which* MARIA JOSEFA *exited, and goes towards the door to the corral. She hesitates there, then takes two more steps.*]

MARTIRIO [*quietly*]: Adela! [*She pauses, then goes closer to the door. Loudly*] Adela!

[ADELA *appears. Her hair is a bit mussed up.*]

ADELA: Why are you looking for me?

MARTIRIO: Stay away from that man!

ADELA: Who are you to tell me that?

MARTIRIO: That's no place for a decent woman!

ADELA: How you'd love to be there yourself!

MARTIRIO [*loudly*]: The time has come for me to speak! Things can't go on like this!

ADELA: This is only the beginning. I had the strength to go forward – the looks and the courage you don't have! I saw death under this roof, and I went out to look for what is mine, what belongs to me!

MARTIRIO: That heartless man came here for someone else. You have come between them!

ADELA: He came for the money, but his eyes were always for me.

MARTIRIO: I won't allow you to snatch him away! He is going to marry Angustias.

ADELA: You know better than I that he doesn't love her.

MARTIRIO: I know.

ADELA: You know, because you've seen that he loves me!

MARTIRIO: Yes.

ADELA [*coming close to her*]: He loves me! He loves me!

MARTIRIO: Stick a knife in me if you like, but don't say that to me again!

ADELA: That's why you're trying to keep me from going off with him. You don't care if he embraces a woman he doesn't love. Me neither. Yes, he could spend a hundred years with

Angustias, but if he embraces me, it seems terrible to you, because you love him, too! You love him!

MARTIRIO [*dramatically*]: Yes! Let me say it openly. Yes! Let my breast explode like a bitter pomegranate! I love him!

ADELA [*impulsively going to embrace her*]: Martirio, Martirio, it's not my fault!

MARTIRIO: Don't embrace me! Don't try to soften my eyes. My blood is no longer your blood! I try to think of you as a sister, but I see you only as a woman! [*She pushes her away.*]

ADELA: There's no solution here. If one of us has to drown, let her drown! Pepe el Romano is mine! He takes me into the reeds at the edge of the river!

MARTIRIO: Never!

ADELA: I can't stand the horror of this house any more, not after knowing the taste of his mouth! I will be what he wants me to be. With the whole town against me, branding me with their fiery fingers, persecuted by people who claim to be decent, and right in front of them I will put on a crown of thorns, like any mistress of a married man!

MARTIRIO: Be quiet!

ADELA: Yes! Yes! [*Quietly*] Let's go to sleep. Let him marry Angustias. I don't care any more. But I will go to a little house, alone, where he will see me whenever he wants, whenever he feels the need.

MARTIRIO: That won't happen as long as I have one drop of blood in my body!

ADELA: Not you – you're weak – I could bring a wild stallion to his knees with the strength in my little finger!

MARTIRIO: Don't raise your voice, I can't stand it! My heart is full of something so vicious I can't keep it from smothering me!

ADELA: They teach us to love our sisters. God must have abandoned me out in the middle of the darkness, because I see you as if I had never seen you before!

[*A* whistle *is heard.* ADELA *runs towards the door, but* MARTIRIO *blocks it.*]

MARTIRIO: Where are you going?

ADELA: Get away from the door!

MARTIRIO: Get past if you can!

ADELA: Get away!

[*They struggle.*]

MARTIRIO [*loudly*]: Mother! Mother!

[BERNARDA *appears, in petticoats and a black shawl.*]

BERNARDA: Stop it! Stop it! How poor I am, with no bolt of lightning between my fingers!

MARTIRIO [*pointing at* ADELA]: She was with him! Look at her petticoats, covered with straw!

BERNARDA: That is the bed of sinful women! [*She moves towards* ADELA, *furiously.*]

ADELA [*confronting her*]: The shouting in this prison is over! [*She seizes her mother's cane and breaks it in two.*] This is what I do with the tyrant's rod! Don't take one step more. No one gives me orders but Pepe!

MAGDALENA [*entering*]: Adela!

[PONCIA *and* ANGUSTIAS *enter.*]

ADELA: I am his woman. [*To* ANGUSTIAS] Get that into your head – and go out to the corral and tell him. He will be master of this entire house! He's out there, breathing like a lion!

ANGUSTIAS: My God!

BERNARDA: The gun! Where is the gun?

[BERNARDA *runs out, followed by* MARTIRIO. AMELIA *appears upstage, looking on in terror, her head against the wall.*]

ADELA: No one is going to stop me! [*She starts to leave.*]

ANGUSTIAS [*seizing her*]: You're not leaving here – you and your triumphant body! Thief! You're a dishonour to our house!

MAGDALENA: Let her go where we'll never see her again.

[*A shot is heard.*]

BERNARDA [*entering*]: I dare you to find him now!

MARTIRIO [*entering*]: That's the end of Pepe el Romano!

ADELA: Pepe! My God! Pepe!

[*She runs out of the room.*]

PONCIA: Did you kill him?

MARTIRIO: No. He ran off on his horse.

BERNARDA: It was not my fault. A woman is not trained to use a gun.

MAGDALENA: Then why did you say that?

MARTIRIO: Because of her. I would have poured a river of blood over her head!

PONCIA: Damn you!

MAGDALENA: You're a fiend!

BERNARDA: Though it's better this way.

[*There is a heavy thud.*]

Adela! Adela!

PONCIA [*at the door*]: Open up!

BERNARDA: Open up! Don't think these walls can hide your shame!

MAID [*entering*]: The neighbours are awake!

BERNARDA [*like the low roar of a lion*]: Open up, or I'll break down the door!

[*She pauses. All is silent.*]

Adela! [*She backs away from the door.*] Bring a hammer!

[PONCIA *shoves the door open and enters. Then she screams and runs out.*]

What is it?

PONCIA [*her hands at her throat*]: God keep us from coming to that end!

[*The sisters draw back from the door. The* MAID *crosses herself.* BERNARDA *screams and steps forward.*]

PONCIA: Don't go in!

BERNARDA: No. Not me! Pepe, you may go running off alive, through the shadows of the poplars, but one day you will fall. Cut her down. My daughter has died a virgin. Carry her to her room and dress her in white. No one is to say a thing. She died a virgin. Send word for the bells to toll twice at dawn.

MARTIRIO: She was fortunate a thousand times over – she had him.

BERNARDA: I want no weeping. We must look death in the face. Silence! [*To another* DAUGHTER] Be quiet, I said! [*To another* DAUGHTER] Tears, when you're alone. We will all drown ourselves in a sea of mourning. The youngest daughter of Bernarda Alba has died a virgin. Did you hear me? Silence! Silence, I said! Silence!

CURTAIN

READ MORE IN PENGUIN

In every corner of the world, on every subject under the sun, Penguin represents quality and variety – the very best in publishing today.

For complete information about books available from Penguin – including Puffins, Penguin Classics and Arkana – and how to order them, write to us at the appropriate address below. Please note that for copyright reasons the selection of books varies from country to country.

In the United Kingdom: Please write to *Dept. EP, Penguin Books Ltd, Bath Road, Harmondsworth, West Drayton, Middlesex UB7 0DA*

In the United States: Please write to *Consumer Services, Penguin Putnam Inc., 405 Murray Hill Parkway, East Rutherford, New Jersey 07073-2136.* VISA and MasterCard holders call 1-800-631-8571 to order Penguin titles

In Canada: Please write to *Penguin Books Canada Ltd, 10 Alcorn Avenue, Suite 300, Toronto, Ontario M4V 3B2*

In Australia: Please write to *Penguin Books Australia Ltd, 487 Maroondah Highway, Ringwood, Victoria 3134*

In New Zealand: Please write to *Penguin Books (NZ) Ltd, Private Bag 102902, North Shore Mail Centre, Auckland 10*

In India: Please write to *Penguin Books India Pvt Ltd, 11 Community Centre, Panchsheel Park, New Delhi 110017*

In the Netherlands: Please write to *Penguin Books Netherlands bv, Postbus 3507, NL-1001 AH Amsterdam*

In Germany: Please write to *Penguin Books Deutschland GmbH, Metzlerstrasse 26, 60594 Frankfurt am Main*

In Spain: Please write to *Penguin Books S. A., Bravo Murillo 19, 1°B, 28015 Madrid*

In Italy: Please write to *Penguin Italia s.r.l., Via Vittorio Emanuele 45la, 20094 Corsico, Milano*

In France: Please write to *Penguin France, 12, Rue Prosper Ferradou, 31700 Blagnac*

In Japan: Please write to *Penguin Books Japan Ltd, Iidabashi KM-Bldg, 2-23-9 Koraku, Bunkyo-Ku, Tokyo 112-0004*

In South Africa: Please write to *Penguin Books South Africa (Pty) Ltd, P.O. Box 751093, Gardenview, 2047 Johannesburg*

READ MORE IN PENGUIN

Published or forthcoming:

Ulysses   James Joyce

Written over a seven-year period, from 1914 to 1921, *Ulysses* has survived bowdlerization, legal action and bitter controversy. An undisputed modernist classic, its ceaseless verbal inventiveness and astonishingly wide-ranging allusions confirm its standing as an imperishable monument to the human condition. 'Everybody knows now that *Ulysses* is the greatest novel of the century' Anthony Burgess, *Observer*

Nineteen Eighty-Four   George Orwell

Hidden away in the Record Department of the Ministry of Truth, Winston Smith skilfully rewrites the past to suit the needs of the Party. Yet he inwardly rebels against the totalitarian world he lives in, which controls him through the all-seeing eye of Big Brother. 'His final masterpiece . . . *Nineteen Eighty-Four* is enthralling' Timothy Garton Ash, *New York Review of Books*

The Day of the Locust *and* **The Dream Life of Balso Snell**
Nathanael West

These two novellas demonstrate the fragility of the American dream. In *The Day of the Locust*, talented young artist Todd Hackett has been brought to Hollywood to work in a major studio. He discovers a surreal world of tarnished dreams, where violence and hysteria lurk behind the glittering façade. 'The best of the Hollywood novels, a nightmare vision of humanity destroyed by its obsession with film' J. G. Ballard, *Sunday Times*

The Myth of Sisyphus   Albert Camus

The Myth of Sisyphus is one of the most profound philosophical statements written this century. It is a discussion of the central idea of absurdity that Camus was to develop in his novel *The Outsider*. Here Camus poses the fundamental question – Is life worth living? – and movingly argues for an acceptance of reality that encompasses revolt, passion and, above all, liberty.

READ MORE IN PENGUIN

Published or forthcoming:

A Confederacy of Dunces John Kennedy Toole

A monument to sloth, rant and contempt, a behemoth of fat, flatulence and furious suspicion of anything modern – this is Ignatius J. Reilly of New Orleans. In magnificent revolt against the twentieth century, he propels his monstrous bulk among the flesh-pots of a fallen city, a noble crusader against a world of dunces. 'A masterwork of comedy' *The New York Times*

Giovanni's Room James Baldwin

Set in the bohemian world of 1950s Paris, *Giovanni's Room* is a landmark in gay writing. David is casually introduced to a barman named Giovanni and stays overnight with him. One night lengthens to more than three months of covert passion in his room. As he waits for his fiancée to arrive from Spain, David idealizes his planned marriage while tragically failing to see Giovanni's real love.

Breakfast at Tiffany's Truman Capote

It's New York in the 1940s, where the Martinis flow from cocktail-hour to breakfast at Tiffany's. And nice girls don't, except, of course, Holly Golightly. Pursued by Mafia gangsters and playboy millionaires, Holly is a fragile eyeful of tawny hair and turned-up nose. She is irrepressibly 'top banana in the shock department', and one of the shining flowers of American fiction.

Delta of Venus Anaïs Nin

In *Delta of Venus* Anaïs Nin conjures up a glittering cascade of sexual encounters. Creating her own 'language of the senses', she explores an area that was previously the domain of male writers and brings to it her own unique perceptions. Her vibrant and impassioned prose evokes the essence of female sexuality in a world where only love has meaning.

READ MORE IN PENGUIN

Published or forthcoming:

A Clockwork Orange Anthony Burgess

Fifteen-year-old Alex enjoys rape, drugs and Beethoven's Ninth. He
and his gang rampage through a dystopian future, hunting for terrible
thrills, until he finds himself at the mercy of the state and the minis-
trations of Dr Brodsky, the government psychologist. *A Clockwork
Orange* is both a virtuoso performance from an electrifying prose
stylist and a serious exploration of the morality of free will.

On the Road Jack Kerouac

On the Road swings to the rhythms of 1950s underground America,
with Sal Paradise and his hero Dean Moriarty, traveller and mystic,
the living epitome of Beat. Now recognized as a modern classic, its
American Dream is nearer that of Walt Whitman than F. Scott
Fitzgerald, and it goes racing towards the sunset with unforgettable
exuberance, poignancy and autobiographical passion.

Zazie in the Metro Raymond Queneau

Impish, foul-mouthed Zazie arrives in Paris from the country to stay
with her female-impersonator Uncle Gabriel. All she really wants to
do is ride the metro, but finding it shut because of a strike, Zazie looks
for other means of amusement and is soon caught up in a comic
adventure that becomes wilder and more manic by the minute.
Queneau's cult classic is stylish, witty and packed full of wordplay and
phonetic games.

Lolita Vladimir Nabokov

Poet and pervert Humbert Humbert becomes obsessed by twelve-
year-old Lolita and seeks to possess her, first carnally and then
artistically. This seduction is one of many dimensions in Nabokov's
dizzying masterpiece, which is suffused with a savage humour and rich
verbal textures. 'You read Lolita sprawling limply in your chair,
ravished, overcome, nodding scandalized assent' Martin Amis

READ MORE IN PENGUIN

Published or forthcoming:

Seven Pillars of Wisdom T. E. Lawrence

Although 'continually and bitterly ashamed' that the Arabs had risen in revolt against the Turks as a result of fraudulent British promises, Lawrence led them in a triumphant campaign. *Seven Pillars of Wisdom* recreates epic events with extraordinary vividness. However flawed, Lawrence is one of the twentieth century's most fascinating figures. This is the greatest monument to his character.

A Month in the Country J. L. Carr

A damaged survivor of the First World War, Tom Birkin finds refuge in the village church of Oxgodby where he is to spend the summer uncovering a huge medieval wall-painting. Immersed in the peace of the countryside and the unchanging rhythms of village life, Birkin experiences a sense of renewal. Now an old man, he looks back on that idyllic summer of 1920.

Lucky Jim Kingsley Amis

Jim Dixon has accidentally fallen into a job at one of Britain's new redbrick universities. A moderately successful future beckons, as long as he can survive a madrigal-singing weekend at Professor Welch's, deliver a lecture on 'Merrie England' and resist Christine, the hopelessly desirable girlfriend of Welch's awful son Bertrand. 'A flawless comic novel . . . It has always made me laugh out loud' Helen Dunmore, *The Times*

Under Milk Wood Dylan Thomas

As the inhabitants of Llareggub lie sleeping, their dreams and fantasies deliciously unfold. Waking up, their dreams turn to bustling activity as a new day begins. In this classic modern pastoral, the 'dismays and rainbows' of the imagined seaside town become, within the cycle of one day, 'a greenleaved sermon on the innocence of men'.

READ MORE IN PENGUIN

Published or forthcoming:

Swann's Way Marcel Proust

This first book of Proust's supreme masterpiece, *A la recherche du temps perdu*, recalls the early youth of Charles Swann in the small, provincial backwater of Combray through the eyes of the adult narrator. The story then moves forward to Swann's life as a man of fashion in the glittering world of *belle-époque* Paris. A scathing, often comic dissection of French society, *Swann's Way* is also a story of past moments tantalizingly lost and, finally, triumphantly rediscovered.

Metamorphosis and Other Stories Franz Kafka

A companion volume to *The Great Wall of China and Other Short Works*, these translations bring together the small proportion of Kafka's works that he thought worthy of publication. This volume contains his most famous story, 'Metamorphosis'. All the stories reveal the breadth of Kafka's literary vision and the extraordinary imaginative depth of his thought.

Cancer Ward Aleksandr Solzhenitsyn

One of the great allegorical masterpieces of world literature, *Cancer Ward* is both a deeply compassionate study of people facing terminal illness and a brilliant dissection of the 'cancerous' Soviet police state. Withdrawn from publication in Russia in 1964, it became a work that awoke the conscience of the world. 'Without doubt the greatest Russian novelist of this century' *Sunday Times*

Peter Camenzind Hermann Hesse

In a moment of 'emotion recollected in tranquility' Peter Camenzind recounts the days of his youth: his childhood in a remote mountain village, his abiding love of nature, and the discovery of literature which inspires him to leave the village and become a writer. 'One of the most penetrating accounts of a young man trying to discover the nature of his creative talent' *The Times Literary Supplement*